Today's Glimpse Of Tomorrow's History

Dr. Alton T. Midgett Sr., Th.G., B.R.E., Th.B., M.R.E., Th.M., D.D., Th.D., Ph.D.

Chairman of the Board of Directors, CEO, and Founder of

Global Fundamental Baptist Missions, Inc.
P.O. Box 1195
Newnan, GA 30264

Phone (770) 304-8980

Second Printing
Revised Version 2010

ISBN 978-1-60208-161-1

Printed in the USA by

Faith Baptist Publications

Ft. Pierce, FL 34982

www.fbcpublications.com

TABLE OF CONTENTS

END

Dedication

When praying concerning the writing of this book, I wanted a book that could be easily understood, one with big enough print to be easily read, with a lot of space for notes.

I want to thank my great Master, King, and Savior, the Lord Jesus Christ for salvation by His grace through His shed blood. I wish to thank Him for His great love and mercy that He has given to me and my family, and for my family's faithfulness and dedication to our LORD.

Thanks also to my dear friends Dr. Darrell Hayes, Dr. Steve Harper and his wife Janet, my next door neighbors, brother and sister Fred and Uple Carter for their valuable help with this book, and also those great men and women of God who have gone before us and shared with us what God had given them. Some of their names you will find in this book.

I pray you will enjoy this book, but in everything give God the glory.

Dr. Alton T. Midgett Sr.

Psalms 126: 5-6

Chapter 1

THE BEGINNING

Introduction to the book of Revelation: Formal title, The Revelation of St. John the Divine. We find the name of John in the first chapter of Revelation. John was exiled on the isle of Patmos about A.D. 96.

The Lord Jesus Christ directly revealed to John about things to come in the latter days. It presents more detail of the Tribulation than any other book. These parenthetic passages seem to summarize or to give overview of the greater flow of events as adjunct thoughts. The church is clearly seen in chapter three.

The church disappearing from earthly view is seen again in chapter four, and later the rapture with Christ in chapter nineteen, a pre-tribulation rapture is clearly implied.

The essence of this book is summarized in this succinct statement: "The revelation of Jesus Christ, which God gave unto him, to show unto his servants things which must shortly come to pass." Revelation came from God the Father to Jesus His Son who relayed it to John by an angel.

Let's look at Revelation chapter one verse four, the message to the churches in Asia, and then chapters two and three to the seven churches.

These chapters follow patterns of seven: The seven judgments of great tribulations among all people, the seven trumpet judgments, the seven personalities, the seven vials, the seven thunders, and other information pertaining to the day of the Lord. But through all this, man will have another chance.

These include the Jewish and Gentile remnant of Revelation chapter seven.

Even before the fall of man in the Garden of Eden, God had another place prepared for him. It is a place of such beauty for those who would love Him and serve Him, not because they were made to serve Him, but because they loved Him.

Mankind was given the key to that beautiful new city, and most have rejected it. Jesus [the key] came, died for the sins of all mankind that they would take him as their Lord and Savior, and afterward be with Him at His second coming.

He sent such men as Paul who wrote in order to try to encourage and help others understand the truths of the second coming of Christ, and the reasoning ability God gives us because of this knowledge.

The Church of Thessalonica was becoming idle, giving little or no thought to the coming of Christ. Paul taught that Christ could come at any time, but like most today, their eyes were focused on the material things of their day.

2Thessalonians 2:3-12, "Let no man deceive you by any means: for that day shall not come, except there come a falling away first, and that man of sin be revealed, the son of perdition;" (The son of perdition is Satan, the son of eternal damnation.)

V4. "Who opposeth and exalteth himself above all that is called God, or that is worshipped; so that he as God sitteth in the temple of God, showing himself that he is God.

V5. Remember ye not, that, when I was yet with you, I told you these things?

V6. And now ye know what withholdeth that he might be revealed in his time.

V7. For the mystery of iniquity doth already work: only he who now letteth will let, until he be taken out of the way."
(The bride of Christ must also be taken out of the way.)

V8. "And then shall that Wicked be revealed, whom the Lord shall consume with the spirit of his mouth, and shall destroy with the brightness of his coming:

V9. Even him, whose coming is after the working of Satan with all power and signs and lying wonders,

V10. And with all deceivableness of unrighteousness in them that perish; because they received not the love of the truth, that they might be saved.

V11. And for this cause God shall send them strong delusion, that they should believe a lie:

V12. That they all might be damned who believed not the truth, but had pleasure in unrighteousness."

We can have comfort in knowing that our troubles are not in vain, but will help us to prepare for the kingdom, and are for God's glory.

Paul tells us not to listen to the rumors that the day of the Lord has already begun, and 2Thessalonians 2:3-12 states the things that must happen before the coming of Christ. Now, two thousand years later, we are without a doubt at the door of His coming.

Paul taught that the coming of the Lord would vindicate the

righteous and punish the wicked. Many do not understand the second coming of the Lord; however, let it be clear to anyone who may read these writings that these prophecies are not of my own private interpretation, but of the clear interpretation of Scripture.

In order to keep the order of prophecy, we must go to the very beginning.

In preparing for this writing, I studied many books. One book which I really found helpful was the *Life Application Study Bible (KJV)*, along with the *Franklin Dictionary*.

Some of the quotes I will share with you are from the *King James Study Bible, Matthew Henry's Commentary, Nave's Topical Bible, the Scofield Study Bible*, Dr. H.A. Ironside, Dr. Oliver B. Greene, Dr. Charles Spurgeon, Dr. Harold Sightler, Dr. Hal Lindsey, Dr. Clarence Larkin and various Bible dictionaries. Dr. Sightler was a dear friend and supporter of our ministry in Canada.

At this point I would like to share a thought with you. It has been stated that some of our well known prophecy teachers have lowered their standards, and this could be true. If this is so it truly saddens my heart.

We understand that everyone will not agree with what you and I believe, but we must let God be the judge. Even so it does not take away from their knowledge of prophecy.

It is important to understand that the knowledge given in all books was learned by studying the works of other writers, and comparing them with the Word of God. I praise the Lord for those who have given themselves to the study of His Word.

4

Everything you read here has already been said, but it is my desire to write in a manner that can be easily understood, especially the different teachings concerning the rapture.

There are some who believe, and teach, that the rapture will take place before the Tribulation and the Millennium.

There are those who teach other views. I personally believe in the Pre-Tribulation, Pre-Millennial return of Christ. There are three main views. Let's look at them.

1. The Pre-Tribulation Rapture: Jesus will come before the Tribulation.

2. The Mid-Tribulation Rapture: Jesus will come in the middle of the Tribulation.

3. The Post-Tribulation Rapture: Jesus will come after the Tribulation.

I think it is important to note that there are a lot of good people who are going to differ on this subject. Regardless of what some may think, if they have been born again by the shed blood of our Lord and Savior Jesus Christ, they will go to heaven, and their opinion is not a damnable doctrine just because it may differ with mine or yours.

I also think that it is important that we realize as individuals we will never understand everything about the blessed Word of God.

Let me state again that I believe in the Pre-Tribulation rapture. In short, this belief indicates that Christ will rapture His Church to the Father before the Tribulation begins.

Let me also state that I believe the Scripture from the literal view of Bible interpretation. If one interprets Scripture literally, and consistently, I feel he will arrive at the conclusion that the Church will be removed before the Tribulation begins.

In chapters one through three in the book of The Revelation, the Church is mentioned nineteen times as being on earth. However, later chapters of Revelation, chapters four through nineteen which describe the Tribulation period, make no mention of the Church being on earth during the wrath of God.

The next time we find the Church is in Revelation 19:7-9, at the Marriage of the Lamb.

This is also found in 2Corinthians 5:10, where every believer must appear before the Judgment Seat of Christ.

As we look at this we can understand why some disagree. Paul faced this problem. He had to deal with the Thessalonians, and in teaching them there were some who misunderstood. There is only one who can teach of things past, present, and future with full understanding and without error, and He is the Lord Jesus Christ.

In Revelation chapter one, verse one, we find our teacher, Jesus, showing John what he should write:

Revelation 1:1-3, "The Revelation of Jesus Christ, which God gave unto him, to shew unto his servants things which must shortly come to pass; and he sent and signified it by his angel unto his servant John:

V2. Who bare record of the word of God, and of the testimony of Jesus Christ, and of all things that he saw.

6

V3. Blessed is he that readeth, and they that hear the words of this prophecy, and keep those things which are written therein: for the time is at hand."

So, all Revelation comes through our Lord Jesus Christ. It is through Jesus that we receive knowledge, and are directed in what we should and should not do. Not only is Christ our teacher, He is also the mediator between God and man.

1Timothy 2:3-6, "For this is good and acceptable in the sight of God our Savior;

V4.Who will have all men to be saved, and to come unto the knowledge of the truth.

V5. For there is one God, and one mediator between God and men, the man Christ Jesus;

V6. Who gave himself a ransom for all, to be testified in due time."

I need to point out at this time that Jesus takes His instructions from His Father. We are told by Jesus that He came to do the will of His Father.

Nowhere in Scripture do we find the importance of Jesus more than in Revelation chapter five, verses one through eight. There He shows us things to come. There we find the "Scroll with Seven Seals", and the only one who was worthy to open the book: The Lion of the tribe of Judah - JESUS. He is the root of David.

Isaiah 11:1-10, "And there shall come forth a rod out of the stem of Jesse, and a Branch shall grow out of his roots:

V2. And the spirit of the LORD shall rest upon him, the spirit of wisdom and understanding, the spirit of counsel and might, the spirit of knowledge and of the fear of the LORD;

V3. And shall make him of quick understanding in the fear of the LORD: and he shall not judge after the sight of his eyes, neither reprove after the hearing of his ears:

V4. But with righteousness shall he judge the poor, and reprove with equity for the meek of the earth: and he shall smite the earth with the rod of his mouth, and with the breath of his lips shall he slay the wicked.

V5. And righteousness shall be the girdle of his loins, and faithfulness the girdle of his reins.

V6. The wolf also shall dwell with the lamb, and the leopard shall lie down with the kid; and the calf and the young lion and the fatling together; and a little child shall lead them.

V7. And the cow and the bear shall feed; their young ones shall lie down together: and the lion shall eat straw like the ox.

V8. And the sucking child shall play on the hole of the asp, and the weaned child shall put his hand on the cockatrice' den.

V9. They shall not hurt nor destroy in all my holy mountain: for the earth shall be full of the knowledge of the LORD, as the waters cover the sea.

V10. And in that day there shall be a root of Jesse, which shall stand for an ensign of the people; to it shall the Gentiles seek: and his rest shall be glorious. "

Matthew 22:41-46, "While the Pharisees were gathered together, Jesus asked them,

V42. Saying, What think ye of Christ? Whose son is He? They say unto him, The Son of David.

V43. He saith unto them, How then doth David in spirit call him Lord, saying,

V44. The LORD said unto my Lord, Sit thou on my right hand, till I make thine enemies thy footstool?

V45. If David then call him Lord, how is he his son?

V46. And no man was able to answer him a word, neither durst any men from that day forth ask him any more questions."

What a promise that God will take care of our enemies. Satan and all his demons and followers will be cast off into the LAKE OF FIRE.

Chapter 2

PROPHECY PROVEN

I know that there are those who will wonder why I put this chapter in a prophecy book such as this.

When God first spoke to man concerning the translation of His word, He stated in Genesis chapter one, "In the beginning, GOD." He wanted us to know and understand that His word came only from Him.

Not only that, but God wanted us to know the difference in His terminology, the difference between a certain true saying and a parable.

God uses parables to illustrate through fictional stories. He uses names of people, places, or things when illustrating a truth, a real happening.

In the chapter to follow we are going to look at the Godly and ungodly line from Adam to Christ, from Jesus to the end of the Tribulation, and the Godly line thereafter.

If a person who cannot believe that we serve a God who can reveal the future to others, would he ever believe that which is truly soon coming to pass?

So at this time let's look at some of the things that have happened and prophecies which will come to pass.

Let's look at the prophecies of Isaiah. Isaiah was a prophet who was known for his prophecies concerning the coming of the LORD.

In Isaiah 1:1-31 we read about the vision of Isaiah

concerning Judah and Jerusalem. In verse three, the LORD told them even the ox knew his owner, but Israel did not know.

The prophet, speaking for the LORD, charged them with ingratitude and rebellion. The ox knew its master and the ass his crib. The LORD had given them their every need. But they, like our people today, had turned from Him.

In verses 18-25, God will judge His people and then restore unto them a righteous judge. This was fulfilled in 2Chronicles 36:14-21, Ezekiel 20:33-38, and Jeremiah 23:4-8.

In Jeremiah 1:13-19, because of sin Israel would go into Babylonian captivity. God asked Jeremiah, "What do you see?" Jeremiah said, "I see a boiling pot tilting toward the north." God answered and said that disaster will come from the north upon those that live in the land.

Verses thirteen and fourteen were fulfilled in the Baylonian captivity. But God told Jeremiah not to be terrified and in verse nineteen God said, "I am with thee."

In Jeremiah 2:25-37, Israel was guilty of spiritual harlotry and prostitution. God said I will judge her. Israel said, I have not sinned, she was rebellious, and made new gods.

There were several reasons God put His judgment on Israel.

Jeremiah 2:29- 37, "Wherefore will ye plead with me? ye all have transgressed against me, saith the LORD.

V30. In vain have I smitten your children; they received no correction: your own sword hath devoured your prophets, like a destroying lion.

V31. O generation, see ye the word of the LORD. Have I been a wilderness unto Israel? a land of darkness? wherefore say my people, We are lords; we will come no more unto thee?"

God has led them through the wilderness. He always was and is their light.

V32. "Can a maid forget her ornaments, or a bride her attire? yet my people have forgotten me days without number.

V33. Why trimmest thou thy way to seek love? therefore hast thou also taught the wicked ones thy ways."

If you fellowship with the darkness, you become part of that darkness.

V34. "Also in thy skirts is found the blood of the souls of the poor innocents: I have not found it by secret search, but upon all these.

V35. Yet thou sayest, Because I am innocent, surely his anger shall turn from me. Behold, I will plead with thee, because thou sayest, I have not sinned.

V36. Why gaddest thou about so much to change thy way? thou also shalt be ashamed of Egypt, as thou wast ashamed of Assyria.

V37. Yea, thou shalt go forth from him, and thy hands upon thy head: for the LORD had rejected thy confidences, and thou shall not prosper in them."

Here God is telling Israel thou shalt go forth into captivity in a strange land, with thy hands on thy head for there is no counsel or wisdom in those who cannot prevail against the Lord.

Jeremiah 16:11-13, "Then shalt they say unto them, Because your fathers have forsaken me, saith the LORD, and have walked after other gods, and have served them, and have worshipped them, and have for forsaken me, and have not kept my law;

V12. And ye have done worse than your fathers; for, behold, ye walk every one after the imagination of his evil heart, that they may not harken unto me:

V13. Therefore will I cast you out of this land into a land that you know not, neither ye nor your fathers; and there shall ye serve other gods day and night; where I will not shew you favor."

In Jeremiah 19:1-6, Jesus said he would break Israel and destroy their land as the clay has been broken. God put them into the valley and called it the valley of slaughter. He called it the valley of slaughter instead of the valley of Tophet or the valley of the son of Hinnom. In latter verses God describes their destruction. This judgment was fulfilled in the Babylonian captivity.

Jeremiah chapters twenty-one and twenty-two tell of the destruction falling upon Zedekiah, King of Judah. Zedekiah asked Jeremiah to seek help from the LORD against King Nebuchadnezzar of Babylon that maketh war against us.

Now let's look at another prophecy against King Zedekiah of Judah.

Jeremiah 25: 7-11, "Ye have not harkened unto me, saith the LORD; that ye might provoke me to anger with the works of your hands to your own hurt.

V8. Therefore thus saith the LORD of hosts; Because ye have not heard my words,

V9. Behold, I will send and take all the families of the north, saith the LORD, and Nebuchadnezzar the king of Babylon, my servant, and will bring them against this land, and against the inhabitants thereof, and against all these nations round about, and will utterly destroy them, and make them an astonishment, and an hissing, and perpetual desolations.

V10. Moreover I will take from them the voice of mirth," (mirth: gladness and laughter), *"and the voice of gladness, the voice of the bridegroom, and the voice of the bride, the sound of the millstones, and the light of the candle.*

V11. And this whole land shall be a desolation, and an astonishment; and these nations shall serve the king of Babylon seventy years."

If you begin counting the years from 586 B.C. when Nebuchadnezzar and the Babylonians conquered Jerusalem and carried the people captive to Babylon until the time of their return, it was exactly seventy years.

The Babylonian Empire covered essentially the same area as the Assyrian Empire. After seventy years of captivity, a remnant of the Jews returned to their land to rebuild the temple and the city of Jerusalem around 516 B.C.

I think it would be good at this time to look at Jeremiah 25:12. Because of turning from God, Babylon suffered almost the same fate as Judah. But in further studies Babylon will never recover as Judah has and is continuing to do.

In verse five of chapter twenty-one God said, *"And I myself will fight against you with an outstretched hand and with a strong arm, even in anger, and in fury, and in great wrath."*

This prophecy concerning Judah and King Zedekiah was fulfilled in 2Chronicles 36:15-16.

Prophecy: Satan Destroyer

Genesis 3:15, "And I will put enmity between thee and the woman, and between thy seed and her seed; it shall bruise thy head, and thou shalt bruise his heel."

Fulfillment: *Galatians 4:4-5, "But when the fulness of the time was come, God sent forth his Son, made of a woman, made under the law."*

V5. To redeem them that were under the law, that we might receive the adoption of sons."

Prophecy: Seed of Abram

Genesis 12:1-3, "Now the LORD had said unto Abram, Get thee out of thy country, and from thy kindred, and from thy father's house, unto a land that I will show thee:

V2. And I will make of thee a great nation, and I will bless thee, and make thy name great; and thou shall be a blessing:

V3. And I will bless them that bless thee, and curse him that curseth thee: and in thee shall all families of the earth be blessed."

Fulfillment: *Matthew 1:1, "The book of the generation of Jesus Christ, the son of David, the son of Abraham."*

And I would like to add for my joy, THE SON OF GOD.

Prophecy: Luke 1:18-38. A child shall be born of a virgin.
Fulfillment: Luke 2:1-14.

I have looked up forty Scriptures on the prophesying of events and their fulfillment.

Now let's look at some parables as told by the Lord.

1. The prodigal son.

   "And he said, A certain man had two sons..." Luke 15:11. Again, if he had used a name it would have been real. Remember, in a parable Jesus never used the name of a person.

2. The house built upon a rock (Matthew 7:24:27).

3. The laborers in the vineyard (Matthew 20: 1-16).

These are just a few out of over forty examples.

Chapter 3

FROM ADAM TO THE CROSS

Cain and the sons of Cain, show the difference between the Godly line and the ungodly line from Adam to the cross. The first eleven chapters of Genesis deal with the history of the human race.

The last thirty-nine chapters deal with the family of Abraham. Through this study we will see where some of the nations came from which go against Jesus and ultimately against antichrist at Armageddon.

Adam and Eve were put out of the Garden of Eden because of their rebellion toward God by taking of the forbidden fruit of the Tree of Knowledge.

They had two sons, Cain and Able. Cain murdered Able and allowed Satan to put hate and jealousy in his heart, and then he tried to cover his murder with a lie. God asked, "Where is Able thy brother?" Cain answered, "I know not: Am I my brother's keeper?" Sin cannot be hidden from God.

Genesis 3:13-14, "And the LORD God said unto the woman, What is this that thou hast done? And the woman said, the serpent beguiled me, and I did eat.

V14. And the LORD God said unto the serpent, Because thou hast done this, thou art cursed above all cattle, and above every beast of the field; upon thy belly shalt thou go, and dust shalt thou eat all the days of thy life..."

In Genesis 4:13-14 Cain was driven out of his land, and we can find nowhere in Scripture where Cain repented of his crime. He was sad only because of his punishment, and he remained defiant in his attitude and even defiant toward God.

Genesis 4:9, "And the LORD said unto Cain, Where is Able thy brother? And he said, I know not: Am I my brother's keeper?"

In Genesis 4:17, Cain had Enoch who was his eldest son. Cain built a city east of Eden in the land of Nod, which was the name given to the country where Cain fled. Nod was a country of unrest.

Jared's son, Enoch, walked with God three hundred and sixty five years, and God took him (Genesis 5:24).

Enoch had Irad, Cain's grandson, (Genesis 4:18), which means "Runner or Wild Ass", who was one of the antediluvian patriarchs. After searching many commentaries, I found nothing substantial concerning Irad, except for a brief comment in John Gill's commentary.

Enoch was Irad's father, but little mention is made of him in either Sacred or profane history.

Lamech, "The Wild Man", was the fifth descendant of Cain. He was the first to violate the primeval ordinance of marriage (Genesis 4:23).

Lamech was a sullen, self-willed, haughty, vindictive man, and defiant toward God (Genesis 4:23-24). He also was a murderer like his father Cain (Genesis 4:10).

It would be good to note here that Noah, whose evil father was Lamech, was the start of the Godly generation, which began before the flood and continued after the flood.

Mankind was divided into two branches. Those who abode in the presence of God and those who had fled from Him.

In Genesis 5:1-5, and also in Genesis 4:25, the Godly generation of Adam begins. Genesis 9:26 states: *"And he said, Blessed be the LORD God of Shem; and Canaan shall be his servant."*

The Messianic line came through Seth, Enoch, Eber, Abraham, and eventually to Jesus Christ. Let's look at more Scripture.

Genesis 5:3, "And Adam lived an hundred and thirty years, and begat a son IN HIS OWN LIKENESS," (THE GODLY LINE), *"AFTER HIS IMAGE; AND CALLED HIS NAME SETH."* Seth is part of the genealogy of Jesus.

Luke 3:38 states: *"Which was the son of Enos, which was the son of Seth, which was the son of Adam, which was the son of God."*

God's chosen nation, Israel, would descend through Shem (Genesis 11:10-27; Matthew 1:12-17); thus, through Shem God would meet the spiritual needs of mankind.

Now we have seen the Godly line before the flood, and the generation after the flood. God made a covenant with Noah, his sons, and every living creature that was with him in the ark, that He would never again destroy the earth by a flood. This covenant is for perpetual generations.

Matthew 1:17, "So the generations Abraham to David were fourteen generations; and from David until the carrying away into Babylon are fourteen generations; and from the carrying away into Babylon unto Christ are fourteen generations."

21

Matthew 1:1-16. Here are the names from Abraham to David.

1. Abraham begat Isaac
2. Isaac begat Jacob
3. Jacob begat Judas
4. Judas begat Phares
5. Phares begat Esrom
6. Esrom begat Aram
7. Aram begat Aminadad
8. Aminadad begat Naasson
9. Naasson begat Salmon
10. Salmon begat Booz
11. Booz begat Obed
12. Obed begat Jesse
13. Jesse begat David
14. David

The generation from David to the carrying away of Israel to Babylon.

1. Solomon begat Roboam
2. Roboam begat Abia
3. Abia begat Asa
4. Asa begat Josaphat
5. Josaphat begat Joram
6. Joram begat Ozias
7. Ozias begat Joatham
8. Joatham begat Achaz
9. Achaz begat Ezekias
10. Ezekias begat Manasses
11. Manasses begat Amon
12. Amon begat Josias
13. Josias begat Jechonias
14. Jechonias

Now we have seen the Godly line before the flood, and the Godly generation after the flood to Jechonias.

Many times I have been asked the question, "Who were the sons of God the Bible talks about in Genesis 6:4?" Like most of you I have heard many different answers to this question. For the truth we must go back to the Word of God. I will quote what I found in the *King James Study Bible*.

Genesis 6:1-4, "And it came to pass, when men began to multiply on the face of the earth, and daughters were born unto them,

V2. That the sons of God saw the daughters of men that they were fair; and they took them wives of all which they chose.

V3. And the LORD said, My spirit shall not always strive with man, for that he also is flesh: yet his days shall be an hundred and twenty years.

V4. There were giants in the earth in those days; and also after that, when the sons of God came in unto the daughters of men, and they bare children to them, the same became mighty men which were of old, men of renown."

The "sons of God" (The Hebrew is: בֵּן אלהים *Ben Elohim*) mentioned refers to the Godly line of Seth, which intermarried with the daughters of men, or the ungodly line of Cain.

The result was an ungodly relationship between the lost and saved, a mixed marriage. This relationship brought the wrath of God down upon the world.

Some teach that these "sons of God" were the fallen angels

who married the daughters of men. If God's Word is true, AND IT IS, THIS CAN'T BE.

Let's look at *Matthew 22:30, "For in the resurrection they neither marry, nor are given in marriage, BUT ARE AS THE ANGELS OF GOD IN HEAVEN."*

NOTICE AGAIN WHAT THE SCRIPTURE IS SAYING, *"BUT ARE AS THE ANGELS OF GOD IN HEAVEN."*

You might say BUT, BUT, what about Genesis 6:2. THE BIBLE STATES, WE WILL BE AS THE ANGELS, NOT MARRIED, OR GIVEN IN MARRIAGE.

WOULD GOD HAVE A DIFFERENT STANDARD IN HEAVEN THAN ON EARTH CONCERNING SIN? SEX WITHOUT MARRIAGE IS SIN. EVERY VERSE WE FIND IN THE BIBLE REFERS TO THE ANGELS AS BEING MASCULINE.

Really, this makes no difference to me concerning fellowship, because it is not a teaching that would prevent someone from being saved. Most who teach that angels came and mated with the daughters of men use Job 1:6 which states, *"Now there was a day when the sons of God came to present themselves before the LORD, and Satan came also among them."*

These were the angels of God, made in heaven, not part of the human genealogy. In the Scripture above we see the Godly line through men, and the ungodly line. Also note that it is in this Scripture that the devil is called Satan, which means accuser, for the first time.

Now let's look at the covenants. As we look at this word covenant, it means an agreement that binds two parties together. God made six covenants with promises, of which five are unconditional and everlasting, and one, the Mosaic covenant, which is conditional.

God's covenant with Noah is found in Genesis 6:18, *"But with thee will I establish my covenant; and thou shalt come into the ark, thou, and thy sons, and thy wife, and thy sons' wives with thee."*

This is the first place I could find the word covenant mentioned in the Bible. God promised to put Noah and his family in a place of safety. The six covenants of God are as follows:

1. The Noahic Covenant (Genesis 9:12).

2. The Abrahamic Covenant (Genesis 15).

3. The Mosaic Covenant, which is binding to the new nation of Israel (Exodus 3:4-27 and Exodus 19:18-24).

4. The Davidic Covenant, which is fulfilled in Jesus Christ as the promised seed of David (2Samuel 7:16).

5. The New Covenant, which is unconditional through which God extends His grace to the Gentiles through Jesus Christ (Hebrews 8:8).

6. The Priestly Covenant, because of Phinehas' loyalty to God (Numbers 25:7-13).

Through the New Covenant God promised Phinehas that He would give him and his descendants the covenant of an everlasting priesthood, which was fulfilled through Jesus Christ.

The covenant God made with Noah in Genesis 9:12 involved the dispensation of Human Government, which allowed humanity to govern itself. Man was responsible for governing the world God created.

Under this covenant, man's relationship to the order of nature was confirmed (verse eleven), human government was established, and God promised never again to use a universal flood to judge the world. The dispensation of Human Government culminated with the building of the tower of Babel, and resulted in the judgment of the confusion of tongues.

Genesis 11:1-9, "And the whole earth was of one language, and of one speech.

V2. And it came to pass, as they journeyed from the east, that they found a plain in the land of Shinar; and they dwelt there.

V3. And they said one to another, Go to, let us make brick, and burn them throughly. And they had brick for stone, and slime had they for morter.

V4. And they said, Go to, let us build us a city and a tower, whose top may reach unto heaven; and let us make us a name, lest we be scattered abroad upon the face of the whole earth.

V5. And the LORD came down to see the city and the tower, which the children of men builded.

V6. And the LORD said, Behold, the people is one, and they have all one language; and this they begin to do: and now nothing will be restrained from them, which they have imagined to do.

V7. Go to, let us go down, and there confound their language, that they may not understand one another's speech.

V8. So the LORD scattered them abroad from thence upon the face of all the earth: and they left off to build the city.

V9. Therefore is the name of it called Babel; because the LORD did there confound the language of all the earth: and from thence did the LORD scatter them abroad upon the face of all the earth."

Chapter 4

THE GENERATIONS FROM
THE DESCENDANTS OF NOAH

The sons of Noah after the flood were Shem, Ham, and Japheth. Many of the Asiatic nations descended from Japheth; and these Asiatic nations will fight against Christ in the battle of Armageddon.

The Ungodly Generation of the Sons of Japheth

Japheth is thought by some to be the same as the Greek giant-hero, Iapetos, father of Prometheus, who was regarded by the Greeks as the father of the human race.

There is no evidence that any connection between the Greek Iapetos and the Hebrew Japheth exists. Japheth had sons named Gomer, Magog, Madai, Javan, Tubal, Meshech, and Tiras.

Gomer was the first son of Japheth according to Ezekiel 38:6, which states: *"Gomer, and all his bands"* (bands means crowds of troops*); "the house of Togarmah of the north quarters, and all his bands: and many people with thee."*

Gomer and his descendants formed the prince branch of the population of southeastern Europe. He is generally regarded as the ancestor of the Celtae and the Cimmerii, who in early times settled to the north of the Black Sea and gave their name to the Crimea, the ancient Chersonesus.

In the seventh century B.C. the Crimea were driven out of their original seat by the Scythians and overran western Asia Minor. Some believe that the Latin father Jerome believed that the Scythians were a nation of fierce and innumerable inhabitants, located beyond the Caucasus and Lake Macotis, which met the Caspian Sea and flows outward to India.

They reappear in the time of Rome as the British Cimbri of the north and west of Europe. They crossed the British Isles where their descendants are still found.

Magog, the second son of Japheth according to Ezekiel 38:2 and 39:6, is the same nation that will fight against the LORD JESUS CHRIST.

Ezekiel 38:2, "Son of man, set thy face against Gog, the land of Magog, the chief prince of Meshech and Tubal, and prophesy against him."

Remember, Magog was the son of Japheth, and the grandson of Noah (Gen. 10:2). Some have connected Gog with a Lydian king in western Anatolia named Gyges, and Magog with the Anatolian Scythians.

There has been no end to suggestions as to the identity of Gog and Magog, especially by the Tarters and Turks. Notice that each nation mentioned here lies north of Israel.

Because of this, many teach that the country which will come down from the north to attack Israel will be Russia.

Magog's allies will be Persia (Iran), Ethiopia, Libya, and the tribes of Turkey and Armenia: Meshech, Tubal, Gomer, and Togarmah.

These nations will be listed again in future chapters, and the battle itself will be described in some detail, including the defeat of Gog in Ezekiel 38:17 and 39:8.

It would help the reader to read the whole chapter of Ezekiel 39.

Ezekiel 39:6-7, "And I will send a fire on Magog, and among them that dwell carelessly in the isles: and they shall know that I am the LORD.

V7. So will I make my holy name known in the midst of my people Israel; and I will not let them pollute my holy name any more: and the heathen shall know that I am the LORD, the Holy One in Israel."

Madai is the third son of Japheth. This is the name by which the Medes are known on Assyrian monuments.

Strong's Lexicon states that they inhabited the territory of Media, which was located northwest of Persia proper, southwest of the Caspian Sea, east of Assyria, and west-northwest of the salt desert of Iran.

Javan was the forth son of Japheth whose descendants settled in Greece. Leonia bore the name Javan in Hebrew. Alexander the Great is called the king of "Javan" which is rendered "Grecia" and the rough goat is the king of Grecia: and the great horn that is between his eyes is the first king (Dan. 8:21, 10:20; Zech 9:13).

Tubal was the fifth son of Japheth. He and his descendants settled in Asia Minor.

Meshach was the sixth son of Japheth (Genesis 10:2). He was the founder of a barbarian tribe (Ezek. 27:13, 38:2-3). They were the Moschi, a people inhabiting the Meshech Mountains between the Black and the Caspian Sea.

Psalms 120:5, "Woe is me, that I sojourn in Mesech, that I dwell in the tents of Kedar!"

During the ascendancy of the Babylonians and Persians in Western Asia, the Moschi were subdued. They became the Muscoys, and gave that name to the Russian nation.

The Ungodly Generation of Ham

The sons of Ham were Cush, Mizraim, Put, and Canaan (Genesis, chapter six).

From Cush and Mizraim came the Ethiopians and Egyptians. Knowing where this family migrated is very important if we are going to trace its place in future events.

Cush lived in ancient Ethiopia. His descendants not only lived in Africa, but also were found in the whole of southeastern Asia, and finally settled in Arabia.

Arabia will be another one of the nations that will come down against our Lord. Some of Cush's descendants mingled with the Semites and adopted their language.

Also, some of Cush's descendants dwelt in Hadhramaut, whose chief city was called Sabetha or Sabot. This area at that time was called southeastern Arabia.

The Ethiopians of Caramonia dwelt to the east of the Persian Gulf, and Nimrod, the mighty hunter, was the founder of the first imperial kingdom.

He was renowned for bold and daring deeds. The name Nimrod itself means "we will revolt", which points out his violent resistance against God.

Nimrod was also the builder of the tower of Babel, and God

knows the well-known city of Babylon as a symbol of hostility.

Now let's look at the spread of Ham's children and the country they occupied.

They migrated to the present ruins of Warka, one-hundred miles journey to the southeast of Babel, to a place not determined between Erech and Calneh.

They started four cities in the land of Shinar, now a great heap of ruins seventy-five miles northeast of Babel of the province of Babylon, on the lower Euphrates and Tigris. Nimrod also went to Assyria, a country east of the Tigris, and built four cities.

Ham's children built Rehoboth, Chemosh, and Resen near Nineveh. A large number of towns came from Chemosh. Nimrod probably connected these cities and formed a great capital, possibly the chief fortress of his kingdom on the Tigris.

The Godly Lineage of Shem

Genesis 10:21, "Unto Shem also, the father of all the children of Eber, the brother of Japheth the elder, even to him were children born."

In his stock the Church was preserved; therefore, Moses stops speaking of Japheth and Ham, and speaks of Shem extensively of whom came the Hebrews or Jews.

Genesis 10:21 gives us the record of the sons of Shem. Shem was the brother of Japheth and Ham, and the father of Arpahxad, Elam, Asshur, Lud, Aram, and of course their children and descendants.

Genesis 10:32, "These are the families of the sons of Noah, after their generations, in their nations: and by these were the nations divided in the earth after the flood."

Now let's look at Terah the father of Abram, Haran, and Nahor. Abram was not the oldest, but is mentioned first since God chose him for the messianic line. The name Abram means "Exalted Father."

This signified his honored status as progenitor of God's chosen people. Later his name would be changed to Abraham, which means "Father of a Great Multitude." Abraham was born in approximately 2165 B.C.

Terah, the father of Abram, moved from Ur to Haran where he died.

After the death of his father, Abraham went to Shechem through Zoan to Beer-sheba. Note that Abraham was the forefather of both the Jews and the Arabs.

From Adam to Abraham we have looked at what we have called the Godly and ungodly generations. Then we looked back at the descendants of man, and through this we saw where they migrated from and to, and we will soon see the part they will play in the battle of Armageddon.

Now let's look at some of the last of the ungodly generations.

Genesis 10:2-8, "The sons of Japheth; Gomer, and Magog, and Madai, and Javan, and Tubal, and Meshech, and Tiras.

V3. And the sons of Gomer; Ashkenaz, and Riphath, and Togarmah.

V4. And the sons of Javan; Elishah, and Tarshish, Kittim, and Dodanim.

V5. By these were the isles of the Gentiles divided in their lands; every one after his tongue, after their families, in their nations.

V6. And the sons of Ham; Cush, and Mizraim, and Phut, and Canaan.

V7. And the sons of Cush; Seba, and Havilah, and Sabtah, and Raamah, and Sabtechah: and the sons of Raamah; Sheba, and Dedan.

V8. And Cush begat Nimrod: he began to be a mighty one in the earth."

Abraham then moved into the mountains on the east of Bethel, pitched his tent, having Bethel on the west and Hai on the east, then towards Sodom (Gen. 12:8).

Abraham set up an altar in Shechem and then traveled to Bethel and Sodom. In Genesis 23:9 Abraham buys the cave of Machpelah. Dwelling in Hebron, he traveled to Shur, to Gerar, and then back to Hebron.

Now we will see the genealogy from Abraham, the ancient man, to the modern Israel. But through all of this we will see the six dispensations.

1. Innocence: From Adam to the fall

2. Conscience: From the Fall to the Flood

3. Human Government: From the Flood to Abraham

35

4. Promise: From Abraham to Moses (Israel will have its own land.)

5. Law: From Moses to the Cross

6. Grace: From the Cross to the Rapture (The Church Age)

Now the days of Abraham were one hundred and seventy and five years.

The son of promise, Isaac, was blessed of God and dwelt by the well Lahai-roi. Isaac had two sons, Esau and Jacob. Esau was the father of the Edomites, and Jacob was the father of the Israelites, as documented in the Old Testament.

Later in the Scripture, Esau was used as an illustration of the non-elect of God. *"These are the families of the sons of Noah, after their generations, in their nations: and by these were the nations divided in the earth after the flood" (Gen. 10:32).*

The New Testament refers to Esau as a profane person (Hebrews 12:16, 17), and in Genesis 25:34 the Bible states that Esau despised his birthright (cf. Genesis 27:30-40).

Jacob moved his whole family to Egypt at Joseph's request, where Jacob died at over one hundred and thirty years of age. He was buried in the cave of Machpelah, near Hebron.

Genesis 49:29-33, "And he charged them, and said unto them, I am to be gathered unto my people: bury me with my fathers in the cave that is in the field of Ephron the Hittite,

V30. In the cave that is in the field of Machpelah, which is before Mamre, in the land of Canaan, which Abraham bought with the field of Ephron the Hittite for a possession of a burying place.

V31. There they buried Abraham and Sarah his wife; there they buried Isaac and Rebekah his wife; and there I buried Leah.

V32. The purchase of the field and of the cave that is therein was from the children of Heth.

V33. And when Jacob had made an end of commanding his sons, he gathered up his feet into the bed, and yielded up the ghost, and was gathered unto his people."

Jacob had obtained Isaac's blessing as part of the Godly line. We know the life of Joseph, the son of Jacob born of Rachel. He was sold as a servant, put into prison, served a king, used of God, and died in Egypt at one hundred and ten years old.

As we move on into the book of Exodus we are getting closer to the Lord Jesus Christ. Looking at the Godly line from Noah and the settling down of Israel in Egypt, we see the plan of God and the one who would one day lead the Godly line of Israel to their Promised Land.

Now let's look at the book of Ruth. Ruth was a Moabite who married Mahlon of the Judahite family of Elimelech. Widowed and childless, she went with her mother-in-law Naomi to Bethlehem, where she married Boaz.

She bore a son who became the grandfather of King David, the King of Judah, Obed by name, the father of Jesse, and the father of David, through whom Jesus Christ came. Her name appears in Matthew's genealogy of Jesus.

Thus she joined the Godly line with her firm commitment:

"...thy people shall be my people and thy God my God..."
(Ruth 1:16).

Several groups of people and nations were started through Shem, Ham, and Japheth.

SHEM	HAM	JAPHETH
The Hebrews	The Persians	The Greeks
The Chaldeans	The Syrians	The Thracians
The Assyrians	The Canaanites	The Scythians
	The Egyptians	
	The Philistines	
	The Hittites	
	The Amorites	

From Abraham, to David, to Jesus, Shem's descendants were called Semites. Hams descendants settled in Canaan, Egypt, and parts of Africa. Japheth's descendants settled, for the most, part in Europe and Asia Minor.

This next section deals with the covenant God has set up with the "for whosoever will", New Testament, Godly line stating the conditions of salvation.

Romans 10:10 states: "For with the heart man believeth unto righteousness; and with the mouth confession is made unto salvation."

Number one: Man must believe.
Number two: Man must confess.
Number three: Man must receive.
Number four: Man must present.
.

Romans 12:1, "I beseech you therefore, brethren, by

the mercies of God, that ye present your bodies a living sacrifice, holy, acceptable unto God, which is your reasonable service." (This needs no interpretation.)

Number five: Man will transform.

Romans 12:2, "And be not conformed to this world: but be ye transformed by the renewing of your mind, that ye may prove what is that good, and acceptable, and perfect, will of God."

Romans 10:13, "For whosoever shall call upon the name of the Lord shall be saved."

Please note here, and in many other places that I will stress, the fact that the elect spoken of in the Scriptures are the "FOR WHOSOEVER WILL".

In Romans 10:13 "saved" means "to rescue from danger, to guard from destruction, or to redeem from sin". We are being told here not to be conformed to this world and let the world control our thoughts. Instead we are to turn our minds totally over to the Lord.

Also, a renewed heart goes with a renewed mind, and only then will man seek the perfect will of God.

1Thessalonians 5:23 states: *"And the very God of peace sanctify you wholly; and I pray God your whole spirit and soul and body be preserved blameless unto the coming of our Lord Jesus Christ."*

We need a closer look at that statement. Paul said, *"...soul and body be preserved blameless unto the coming of our Lord Jesus Christ."*

Although the Church was young at this point, Paul was telling them how they should live, and that they were to be looking for the coming of the Messiah.

In the Scripture, Paul was a member of the New Testament Godly line. We are told that Saul, who was renamed Paul, was saved and became a servant separated unto the Gospel.

In Ephesians 3:1 Paul stated: *"For this cause I Paul, the prisoner of Jesus Christ for you Gentiles..."*

Paul was literally stating, "I have been arrested by God to preach the Gospel." In this case Paul had set the example to the Gentiles. He was willing to give himself as a willing sacrifice for the Church.

Next, will the Godly line be a judge and judge others? We will look at this now, then more in a later chapter.

1Corinthians 6:1-3, "Dare any of you having a matter against another, go to law before the unjust, and not before the saints?

V2.Do ye not know that the saints shall judge the world?" (He is speaking of the time period of the millennial reign of Christ.) *"and if the world shall be judged by you, are ye unworthy to judge the smallest matters?*

V3. Know ye not that we shall judge angels? how much more things that pertain to this life?"

Daniel 7:22, "Until the Ancient of days came, and judgment was given to the saints of the most High; and the time came that the saints possessed the kingdom."

The Church, the Godly line, will have an everlasting dominion that will take its place at His second coming.

Question - Are you a part of the Godly line, those who have accepted Christ as their savior?

Chapter 5

DRY BONES LIVE AGAIN

We base our knowledge of prophecy from watching Israel, how it began, where it has been, the direction it is going, and where it will end up.

We are saved, not because of what we have done, but because of what the Lord has done. Jesus died on the cross of Calvary, shedding His own blood for the sins of all mankind.

Because of this great sacrifice, we know that after all is over we will live with our LORD forever.

God has used Israel many times in Scripture in order to set an example for all mankind and to be a light to shine before us in order to understand many prophecies of the end times.

Although we don't know the day or the hour of the coming of the Lord Jesus, Scripture clearly tells us that we are not children of darkness. We are not as a blind person stumbling in a strange room.

The Scripture tells us we are children of light, not darkness. If we study His Word and pray, God will enlighten us to His Scripture. He will guide our steps.

Over hundreds of years, God has given us watchmen (prophets and pastors) to look after our spiritual lives; men to preach to us, to teach us the Word of God, and to warn us when we stray.

Ezekiel 33:1-11, "Again the word of the LORD came unto me saying,

V2. Son of man, speak to the children of thy people, and say unto them, When I bring the sword upon a land, if the people of the land take a man of their coasts, and set him for a watchman:

V3. If when he seeth the sword come upon the land, he blow the trumpet, and warn the people;

V4. Then whosoever heareth the sound of the trumpet, and taketh not warning; if the sword come, and take him away, his blood shall be upon his own head."

Now people are hearing us sound the trumpet, but are not listening; but this does not lessen our responsibility to warn them.

V5. "He heard the sound of the trumpet, and took not warning; his blood shall be upon him. But he that taketh warning shall deliver his soul."

Let's jump back now and look at Exodus 9:19 for an example.

In Exodus 9:19-21, Moses was the watchman over the Jews. In verse nineteen, Moses told them to get their cattle out of the fields, that hail would come and all the cattle in the field would die. They did so and not one of their cattle died, but all of Pharaoh's cattle died. People MUST listen today or they too will die.

If you are saved, God has given you a great responsibility. We are to give them the warning. Now back to verse six of Ezekiel 33.

V6. "But if the watchman see the sword come, and blow not the trumpet, and the people be not warned; if the sword

44

come, and take any person from among them, he is taken away in his iniquity; but his blood will I require at the watchman's hand."

It can't get any clearer than this Scripture. He is telling us to warn the people.

V7. "So thou, O son of man, I have set thee a watchman unto the house of Israel; therefore thou shalt hear the word at my mouth, and warn them from me.

V8. When I say unto the wicked, O wicked man, thou shalt surely die; if thou dost not speak to warn the wicked from his way, that wicked man shall die in his iniquity; but his blood will I require at thine hand.

V9. Nevertheless, if thou warn the wicked of his way to turn from it; if he do not turn from his way, he shall die in his iniquity; but thou hast delivered thy soul."

We hear the warning to the wicked, "thou shalt surely die." But if we don't warn them their blood will be on our hands. If we warn them and they do not repent, their blood WILL NOT be on our hands.

V10. Therefore, O thou son of man, speak unto the house of Israel; Thus ye speak, saying, If our transgressions and our sins be upon us, and we pine away in them, how should we then live?

V11. Say unto them, As I live, saith the Lord GOD, I have no pleasure in the death of the wicked; but that the wicked turn from his way and live: turn ye, turn ye from your evil ways; for why will ye die, O house of Israel?"

In verse eleven our Lord pleaded with them through their

watchman: "Say unto them, AS I LIVE…."

Let's look at this statement, "AS I LIVE." In the Old Testament the words, "AS I LIVE" would identify God as "*Adonai*", which means: Proprietor, Master, Ruler, Commander, the mighty Jehovah.

Another word in the Old Testament that proves this is our Lord speaking is the word "*Abhir*", which means, glorious, majestic, mighty, LORD.

Ezekiel 33:20, "Yet ye say, The way of the Lord is not equal. O ye house of Israel, I will judge you every one after his · ways."

After all the rebellion of Israel God will show mercy.

Ezekiel 34:1-2. "And the word of the LORD came unto me saying,

V2. Son of man, prophesy against the shepherds of Israel, prophesy, and say unto them, Thus sayeth the LORD GOD unto the shepherds; Woe be to the shepherds of Israel that do feed themselves! should not the shepherds feed the flocks?"

In verse seven the Lord is talking to all of His preachers, pastors, missionaries, and evangelists.

"Therefore, ye shepherds, hear the word of the LORD…"

In chapter thirty-six, God gives Israel back her land. In chapter thirty-seven we see what happed to Israel because of its rebellion.

The Israelites lost their homeland and were dispersed as a nation into the entire known world, but it became a nation once again.

Ezekiel 37:1-14, "The hand of the LORD was upon me, and carried me out in the spirit of the LORD, and set me down in the midst of the valley which was full of bones,

V2. And caused me to pass by them round about: and, behold, there were very many in the open valley; and, lo, they were very dry.

V3. And he said unto me, Son of man, can these bones live? And I answered, O Lord GOD, thou knowest.

V4. Again he said unto me, Prophesy upon these bones, and say unto them, O ye dry bones, hear the word of the LORD.

V5. Thus saith the Lord GOD unto these bones; Behold, I will cause breath to enter into you, and ye shall live:

V6. And I will lay sinews upon you, and will bring up flesh upon you, and cover you with skin, and put breath in you, and ye shall live; and ye shall know that I am the LORD.

V7. So I prophesied as I was commanded: and as I prophesied, there was a noise, and behold a shaking, and the bones came together, bone to his bone.

V8. And when I beheld, lo, the sinews and the flesh came up upon them, and the skin covered them above: but there was no breath in them.

V9. Then said he unto me, Prophesy unto the wind, prophesy, son of man, and say to the wind, Thus saith the Lord GOD; Come from the four winds, O breath, and breathe upon these slain, that they may live."

In verse one Ezekiel was carried into a valley of dry bones. In verse five, God said these bones shall live. In verse six, God tells the dry bones, I will put flesh upon you and ye shall live. Again, he is talking about Israel. Then God tells who He is: "I am the LORD."

God is saying to us, preach to them, tell them for me. Come like the four winds and preach to them. Here God is talking to us.

V10. "So I prophesied as he commanded me, and the breath came into them, and they lived, and stood up upon their feet, an exceeding great army.

V11. Then he said unto me, Son of man, these bones are the whole house of Israel: behold, they say, Our bones are dried, and our hope is lost: we are cut off for our parts.

V12. Therefore prophesy and say unto them, Thus saith the Lord GOD; Behold, O my people, I will open your graves, and cause you to come up out of your graves, and bring you into the land of Israel.

V13. And ye shall know that I am the LORD, when I have opened your graves, O my people, and brought you up out of your graves,"

These prophecies will soon come to pass. Now let's look at verse 14.

V14. "And shall put my spirit in you, and ye shall live, and I shall place you in your own land: then shall ye know that I the LORD have spoken it, and performed it, saith the LORD."

Ezekiel chapter 39, verses 15-28, deals with the restoration of a united Israel.

In Ezekiel chapters 38-39, we find the prophecy against Gog. We will look at those chapters later, but for now let's go to chapter six.

Chapter 6

WILL THE CHURCH GO THROUGH
THE TRIBULATION PERIOD?

There is a disagreement among many concerning the Church, whether or not it will go through the Tribulation period. Many will break fellowship with someone who disagrees with them, either one way or the other. To make myself clear, I believe in the pre-millennial return of Christ. Those who are preaching otherwise, however, are not preaching a damnable doctrine.

1John 5:11-12, "And this is the record that God hath given to us eternal life, and this life is in his Son.

V12. He that hath the Son hath life; and he that hath not the Son of God hath not life."

Without the Son of God you will go through Tribulation, lost forever.

John 5:24-30, "Verily, verily, I say unto you, He that heareth my word, and believeth on him that sent me, hath everlasting life, and shall not come into condemnation; but is passed from death unto life.

V25. Verily, verily, I say unto you, The hour is coming, and now is, when the dead shall hear the voice of the Son of God: and they that hear shall live.

V26. For as the Father hath life in himself; so hath he given to the Son to have life in himself.

V27. And hath given him authority to execute judgment also, because he is the Son of man.

V28. Marvel not at this: for the hour is coming, in the which all that are in the graves shall hear His voice,

V29. And shall come forth; they that have done good unto the resurrection of life; and they that have done evil, unto the resurrection of damnation.

V30. I can of mine own self do nothing: as I hear, I judge: and my judgment is just; because I seek not mine own will, but the will of the Father which hath sent me."

The dead in Christ will rise first, before the Tribulation.

Revelation 3:10, "Because thou hast kept the word of my patience, I also will keep thee from the hour of temptation, which shall come upon all the world, to try them that dwell upon the earth."

God's Word is true and powerful. Those who keep His Gospel in a time of peace will find Him there in a time of tribulation. He will remove you from all the harrow of the seven year Tribulation period. We will be with our Lord in His glory.

Until our Lord Jesus does come for His bride we must watch for His imminent return.

Luke 21:36, "Watch ye therefore, and pray always, that ye may be accounted worthy to escape all these things that shall come to pass, and to stand before the Son of man."

Luke 21:34, "And take heed to yourselves, lest at any time your hearts be overcharged with surfeiting, and drunkenness, and cares of this life, and so that day come upon you unawares."

James 5:7-8, "Be patient therefore, brethren, unto the coming of the Lord. Behold, the husbandman waiteth for the precious fruit of the earth, and hath long patience for it, until he receive the early and latter rain.

V8. Be ye also patient; establish your hearts: for the coming of the Lord draweth nigh."

Still there is no mention of the Tribulation because it has not happened as yet. The question is asked, "When then?"

Mark 13:33, "Take ye heed, watch and pray: for ye know not when the time is."

1Thessalonians 5:9-10, "For God hath not appointed us to wrath, but to obtain salvation by our Lord Jesus Christ.

V10. Who died for us, that, whether we wake or sleep, we should live together with him."

God said, I have not appointed you to wrath, or tribulation, but joy with Christ Jesus.

2Peter 3:10-13, "But the day of the Lord will come as a thief in the night; in the which the heavens shall pass away with a great noise, and the elements shall melt with fervent heat, the earth also and the works that are therein shall be burned up.

V11. Seeing then that all these things shall be dissolved, what manner of persons ought ye to be in all holy conversation and godliness.

V12. Looking for and hasting unto the coming of the day of God, wherein the heavens being on fire shall be dissolved, and the elements shall melt with fervent heat?

V13. Nevertheless we, according to his promise, look for new heavens and a new earth, wherein dwelleth righteousness. "

Again, we can find nowhere where the Church will see the harrows of the Tribulation. We only find the Church in a place of safety.

2 Thessalonians 2:4-12, "Who opposeth and exalteth himself above all that is called God, or that is worshipped; so that he as God sitteth in the temple of God, shewing himself that he is God" (Satan).

V5. "Remember ye not, that, when I was yet with you, I told you these things?

V6. And now ye know what withholdeth that he" (Satan) *"might be revealed in his time.*

V7. For the mystery of iniquity doth already work: only he who now letteth will let, until he be taken out of the way.

V8. And then shall that Wicked be revealed" (Satan, the antichrist, the false prophet, and all that will follow the great deceiver.), *"whom the Lord shall consume with the spirit of his mouth, and shall destroy with the brightness of his coming"* (Second Coming):

V9. "Even him, whose coming is after the working of Satan with all power and signs and lying wonders,

V10. And with all deceivableness of unrighteousness in them that perish; because they received not the love of the truth, that they might be saved.

V11. And for this cause God shall send them strong delusion, that they should believe a lie:

V12. That they all might be damned who believed not the truth, but had pleasure in unrighteousness."

The Church is gone; the antichrist is deceiving millions; the Tribulation has begun. The world has been warned but has not listened to the warning of our Lord.

Chapter 7

THE EVENTS CONCERNING
THE RAPTURE AND THE ANTICHRIST

Matthew 25:31, "When the Son of man shall come in his glory, and all the holy angels with him, then shall he sit upon the throne of his glory..."

Matthew 24:30-31, "And then shall appear the sign of the Son of man in heaven: and then shall all the tribes of the earth mourn and they" (These people may be alive today.) *"shall see the Son of man coming in the clouds of heaven with power and great glory.*

V3.1 And he shall send his angels with a great sound of a trumpet, and they shall gather together his elect" (The elect is the "FOR WHOSOEVER WILL.") *"from the four winds, from one end of heaven to the other."*

Romans 10:13, "For whosoever shall call upon the name of the Lord shall be saved."

Revelation 11:15, "And the seventh angel sounded; and there were great voices in heaven, saying, The kingdoms of this world are become the kingdoms of our Lord, and of his Christ; and he shall reign for ever and ever."

I Thes.4:17, "Then we which are alive and remain shall be caught up together with them in the clouds, to meet the Lord in the air: and so shall we ever be with the Lord."

God made a promise that the Godly line saints of the first resurrection will reign with Him a thousand years. Again, He is talking about the thousand year millennial reign of Christ.

Revelation 20:5-6, "But the rest of the dead lived not again until the thousand years were finished. This is the first resurrection.

V6. Blessed and holy is he that hath part in the first resurrection: on such the second death hath no power, but they shall be priests of God and of Christ, and shall reign with him a thousand years."

Those who refused to take the mark of the beast will reign with our Lord a thousand years.

I want us to look at another view where some spiritualize the resurrection; though I can find no reason for this teaching.

Some are teaching that the first resurrection is spiritual, taking place in our heart upon salvation, and that the millennium is our spiritual reign with Christ between His first and second coming, and at which time we will be priests of God because Christ reigns in our hearts. Therefore, the second resurrection is the bodily resurrection of all people for judgment.

Others believe the first resurrection occurs after Satan has been set aside; that it is a physical resurrection of believers who will reign with Christ on the earth for a literal one thousand years. The second resurrection occurs at the end of the Tribulation in order to judge unbelievers who have died.

Revelation 21:8, "But the fearful, and unbelieving, and the abominable, and murderers, and whoremongers, and sorcerers, and idolaters, and all liars, shall have their part in the lake which burneth with fire and brimstone: which is the second death."

Let's look at verse six. The first resurrection is the

resurrection of life. The second resurrection is the resurrection of death. Thanks to our great and wonderful God and Father and Jesus His Son, the second death will have no power over the saved.

But those of the second resurrection will stand before the Great White Throne Judgment at the end of the Millennium. These are the wicked dead.

The Lord of Lords and King of Kings at this point will make His judgment of all the peoples of the earth.

In order to help us understand the difference between the rapture, the coming of Christ when He takes His people home to heaven, and His glorious appearance with His saints before the millennial Kingdom here on earth, I want to share with you what I found in the Tim LaHaye *Prophecy Study Bible*, King James Version. I feel that it will be a help to you, as it was to me.

A. The Rapture

When Christ comes for His own is described in John 14:3 which states, *"And if I go and prepare a place for you, I will come again, and receive you unto myself; that where I am, there ye may be also."*

Christ did not go away with the intent of forsaking us, but rather that He might take us up with Him into heaven when He catches the true Church away before bringing vengeance on those who know not God.

Acts 1:11, "...Ye men of Galilee, why stand ye gazing up into heaven? this same Jesus, which is taken up from you into heaven, shall so come in like manner as ye have seen him go into heaven."

These words were spoken to the astonished disciples, but are intended for the entire Church.

In all places of the Scripture, the full comfort of the Church is considered to be the day when God will be all in all. Therefore, that day is called the day of redemption.

In John 14:2-3, Jesus tells us in His Father's house there are many mansions prepared for us and He will come again and receive us unto Himself.

John 14:6-7, "Jesus saith unto him, I am the way, the truth, and the life: no man cometh unto the Father, but by me.

V7. If ye had known me, ye should have known my Father also..."

Let's compare the rapture of the Church with the Second Coming of Christ.

1. Signs Preceding the Rapture

1Thessalonians 5:1-3, "But of the times and the seasons, brethren, ye have no need that I write unto you.

V2. For yourselves know perfectly that the day of the Lord so cometh as a thief in the night.

V3. For when they shall say, Peace and safety; then sudden destruction cometh upon them, as travail upon a woman with child; and they shall not escape."

2. He Comes to Claim the Church

1Corinthians 15:52, "In a moment, in the twinkling of an eye, at the last trump: for the trumpet shall sound, and the dead shall be raised incorruptible, and we shall be changed."

3. He Comes in the Air

1 Thessalonians 4:17, "Then we which are alive and remain shall be caught up together with them in the clouds, to meet the Lord in the air: and so shall we ever be with the Lord."

4. The Tribulation Begins

2Thessalonians 1:6-9, "Seeing it is a righteous thing with God to recompense tribulation to them that trouble you;

V7. And to you who are troubled rest with us, when the Lord Jesus shall be revealed from heaven with his mighty angels.

V8. In flaming fire taking vengeance on them that know not God, and that obey not the gospel of our Lord Jesus Christ.

V9. Who shall be punished with everlasting destruction from the presence of the Lord, and from the glory of his power…"

5. The Saved are Delivered from Wrath

2Thessalonians 1:10, "When he shall come to be glorified in his saints, and to be admired in all them that believe (because our testimony among you was believed) in that day."

6. He is Seen Only by the Church

1Thessalonians 4:17, "Then we which are alive and remain shall be caught up together with them in the clouds, to meet the Lord in the air: and so shall we ever be with the Lord."

The major passage is in 1Thessalonians 4:13-18 concerning the rapture of God's saints. Paul tells of the revelation of the rapture of the Church, that we will meet Jesus in the air.

The graves will be opened, the dead in Christ shall rise first, and we who remain will meet the Lord in the air.

Afterwards, we will go into the Father's house to fulfill the prophecy of *John 14:2-3, "In my Father's house there are many mansions: if it were not so, I would have told you. I go to prepare a place for you.*

V3. And if I go and prepare a place for you, I will come again, and receive you unto myself; that where I am, there ye may be also." (Also see 1Thessalonians 4:13-18.)

B. The Second Coming

1. Signs Precede the Second Coming

Luke 21:11, "And great earthquakes shall be in divers places, and famines, and pestilences; and fearful sights and great signs shall there be from heaven."

2. He Comes with His Bride

Revelation 19:7, "Let us be glad and rejoice, and give honor to him: for the marriage of the Lamb is come, and his wife hath made herself ready."

3. He Comes to the Earth

Zechariah14:4-5, "And his feet shall stand in that day upon the mount of Olives, which is before Jerusalem on the east, and the mount of Olives shall cleave in the midst thereof toward the east and toward the west, and there shall be a very great valley; and half of the mountain shall remove toward the north, and half of it toward the south.

V5. And ye shall flee to the valley of the mountains; for the valley of the mountains shall reach unto Azal: yea, ye shall flee, like as ye fled from before the earthquake in the days of Uzziah king of Judah: and the LORD my God shall come, and all the saints with thee."

4. The Tribulation Ends

Revelation 20:2-3, "And he laid hold on the dragon, that old serpent, which is the Devil, and Satan, and bound him a thousand years.

V3. And cast him into the bottomless pit, and shut him up, and set a seal upon him, that he should deceive the nations no more, till the thousand years should be fulfilled: and after that he must be loosed a little season."

5. The Unsaved Experience God's Wrath

Revelation 6:15, "And the kings of the earth, and the great men, and the rich men, and the chief captains, and the mighty men, and every bondman, and every free man, hid themselves in the dens and in the rocks of the mountains..."

6. Every Eye Shall See Him

(Revelation 19:11-21)

The central theme of prophecy for believers today is Christ coming for His own in what is taught as the rapture of the Church.

The purpose of the rapture is to take the Church to be with

the Lord. The rapture is not mentioned in the Old Testament, but was first revealed by Jesus Himself to His disciples on His last night.

John 14:1, "Let not your heart be troubled: ye believe in God, believe also me."

We must trust God. There is no other way to strengthen and encourage our minds during the great distresses we must endure. We must believe. We must have faith.

John 14:2, "In my Father's house are many mansions: if it were not so, I would have told you. I go to prepare a place for you."

Jesus is saying that there is not only room enough for Him in His Father's house, but there is also room enough for all who believe in Him.

He further states that He would not deceive with a vain hope, but that He would have plainly told His disciples if they could not go where He was going.

This dialogue is an absolute truth by which the Lord comforts His own by declaring to them that His departure into heaven is not for His benefit alone, but also for all who will believe in Him.

He does not depart to reign alone, but to go before and prepare a place for those who believe His message.

John 14:5 and 7, "Thomas saith unto him, Lord, we know not whither thou goest; and how can we know the way?"

V7. "If ye had known me, ye should have known my Father also: and from henceforth ye know him, and have seen him."

It is clearly taught by this verse that to know God and to see God is the same thing, whereas He said before that no man can see God at any time. It is to be understood in this way: without Christ, or were it not through Christ, no man could ever see God, or ever saw God at any time.

The major passage on the rapture is 1Thess 4:13-18 which states,

"But I would not have you to be ignorant, brethren, concerning them which are asleep, that ye sorrow not, even as others which have no hope.

V14. For if we believe that Jesus died and rose again, even so them also which sleep in Jesus will God bring with him.

V15. For this we say unto you by the word of the Lord, that we which are alive and remain unto the coming of the Lord shall not prevent them which are asleep.

V16. For the Lord himself shall descend from heaven with a shout, with the voice of the archangel, and with the trump of God: and the dead in Christ shall rise first:

V17. Then we which are alive and remain shall be caught up together with them in the clouds, to meet the Lord in the air: and so shall we ever be with the Lord.

V18. Wherefore comfort one another with these words."

The third part of the epistle, which is mixed in among the former exhortations, he returns to afterwards. He speaks of mourning for the dead, the manner of the resurrection, and of the latter days. We must take heed that we do not immoderately mourn for the dead, that is, as those do who think that the dead are utterly perished.

A metaphor for death is but a sleep of the body (for He speaks of the faithful) until the Lord comes (1Thessalonians 4:13-18). Paul tells of the sound of the trumpet that will bring the dead in Christ out of their graves to meet the Lord in the air.

The next moment the saved who are still alive will also leave this earth to meet the Lord in the air. Afterwards they will go into heaven in fulfillment of the prophecy of going to the Father's house in our new bodies.

John 14:2-3, "In my Father's house are many mansions: if it were not so, I would have told you. I go to prepare a place for you.

V3. And if I go and prepare a place for you, I will come again, and receive you unto myself; that where I am, there ye may be also."

The New Testament indicates that the rapture is different from the second coming. First, the rapture will take all of the born again into heaven before the Tribulation in the twinkling of an eye.

The second coming of Christ is a movement from heaven to earth that takes place at the end of the Tribulation, not in the twinkling of an eye, but quite possibly over a twenty-four hour period. Jesus will come with armies to the valley of Armageddon.

Matthew 24:29-31, "Immediately after the tribulation of those days shall the sun be darkened, and the moon shall not give her light, and the stars shall fall from heaven, and the powers of the heavens shall be shaken:

V30. And then shall appear the sign of the Son of man in heaven: and then shall all the tribes of the earth mourn, and they shall see the Son of man coming in the clouds of heaven with power and great glory.

V31. And he shall send his angels with a great sound of a trumpet, and they shall gather together his elect from the four winds, from one end of heaven to the other."

The doctrine of the rapture is a simple one. Prophecies regarding the rapture make no mention of angels or attending hosts, and no mention of a judgment on earth to follow.

The second coming however is a complex event that may possibly take place over many hours. I understand I have used this Scripture before, but I feel it will help simplify the coming statement. It is plain by this verse that to know God and to see God is the same thing.

Now, whereas He said before that no man saw God at any time, it is to be understood in this way: without Christ, or were it not through Christ, no man could ever see God, nor has ever seen God at any time. Finally, in all the passages concerning the rapture, a preceding event is never mentioned. In fact, the only reference to the timing of the rapture is that it will occur before the Tribulation.

How close are we to the rapture of the Church?

Let's look at what the Scripture states about our day. Everything will be as it was then.

1. Over fifty percent of all babies are born out of wedlock.

2. Filthy language coming into our homes through the television set and books.

3. Dads and moms no longer care.

4. White people and black people hating each other.

5. Nation against nation, each hating the other and killing one another without any real cause.

2Timothy 3:2-5, "For men shall be lovers of their own selves, covetous, boasters, proud, blasphemers, disobedient to parents, unthankful, unholy,

V3. Without natural affection, trucebreakers, false accusers, incontinent, fierce, despisers of those that are good,

V4. Traitors, heady, highminded, lovers of pleasures more than lovers of God;

V5. Having a form of godliness, but denying the power thereof: from such turn away."

We are no better than those to whom Paul was writing. Today many people are everything that God hates (read Proverbs 6:6-19). Many people are proud, liars, and murderers. They have wicked imaginations and sow discord among the brethren.

On the fourth of September 2008, I was reading what is considered a family magazine in my doctor's office when I came across an advertisement for pornographic videos. I could not believe my eyes.

What is happening in America and around the world is that we are turning our backs on everything Godly. We as

Christians need to help this sinful world understand that what we are seeing is God's end time prophecy being fulfilled.

Paul told Timothy to turn away from false teachers who prey upon silly women laden with sins, pointing out that a "form of godliness" is mere religion without prayer, or a spiritual life ever learning, and never able to come to the knowledge of the truth. Paul is not just talking to Timothy here, but also to you and me.

The parable of the fig tree is no more than this: that the blossoming is a presage of summer. We foresee that summer is coming, not immediately, but at some distance.

We expect March winds and April showers before summer comes; however we are sure it is coming. We can count on it.

Now let's look at two Scriptures that will show us just how close we really are to the coming of our Lord Jesus Christ.

Matthew 24:32-34, "Now learn a parable of the fig tree; When his branch is yet tender, and putteth forth leaves, ye know that summer is nigh:

V33. So likewise ye, when ye shall see all these things, know that it is near, even at the doors.

V34. Verily I say unto you, This generation shall not pass, till all these things be fulfilled."

Now let's look at Luke 21: 29-32. Let's look closely, it may say the same thing, but differently.

V29. "And he spoke to them a parable, Behold the fig tree, AND ALL THE TREES;

*V30. When they now shoot forth, ye see and KNOW of your
own selves that summer is now nigh at hand.*

*V31. So likewise ye, when ye see these things come to pass,
know ye that the kingdom of God is nigh at hand.*

*V32. Verily I say unto you, This generation shall not pass
away till all be fulfilled."*

Some are saying the difference between Matthew 24:32-34
and Luke 21:29-32 is that Matthew twenty-four is not talking
about Israel. Both Scriptures are talking about Israel, but
Luke 21 also includes the gentiles with this statement, "AND
ALL THE TREES."

Events that we are seeing today are indications that Christ is
about to return to earth. Of course, we understand that no
man can know the time of our Lord's return. Still there are
certain things happening to suggest his soon return.

Israel's Return to the Promised Land

I would like to share with you some information I read some
time ago concerning the return of Israel to her land. I
understand that there are some who teach that the Lord must
come shortly after Israel returns to her country.

Please let me state once again, NO ONE KNOWS WHEN
OUR LORD IS COMING. Many of us may think we have
some sure idea of His coming, but no one really knows.

We understand that Israel's return to the Promised Land
starts the last count down to the coming of our Lord Jesus
Christ. Again no one knows the time exact timing of His
coming.

I found a copy of the Declaration of Independence of The State of Israel, Issued at Tel Aviv on May 14, 1948. I would like to share this with you.

The date for statehood was finally set for May 15, 1948. As the occasion approached, Jewish excitement was tempered by threat of war with the Arabs. Arab leaders were promising a war of extermination.

Quoting Israel's Final Holocaust, by Jack Van Impe: "On the morning of May 14, 1948 the British lowered the Union Jack in Jerusalem. By mid-afternoon there was a full scale war on throughout the country between the Arabs and the Jews.

At 4 P.M. that day, David Ben Gurion read the Declaration of Independence of Israel and it was broadcast from the Tel Aviv Museum."

"On November 29, 1947, the General Assembly of the United Nations adopted a Resolution for the establishment of an independent Jewish State in Palestine, and called upon the inhabitants of the country to take such steps as may be necessary on their part to put the plan into effect.

This recognition by the United Nations of the right of the Jewish people to establish their independent state may not be revoked. It is, moreover, the self-evident right of the Jewish people to be a nation, as all other nations, in its own sovereign state.

ACCORDINGLY, WE, the members of the National Council, representing the Jewish people in Palestine and the Zionist movement of the world, met together in solemn assembly today, the day of the termination of the British mandate for Palestine, by virtue of the natural and historic right of the Jewish and of the Resolution of the General Assembly of the United Nations,

HEREBY PROCLAIM the establishment of the Jewish State in Palestine, to be called ISRAEL.

WE HEREBY DECLARE that as from the termination of the Mandate at midnight, this night of the 14th and 15th May, 1948, and until the setting up of the duly elected bodies of the State in accordance with a Constitution, to be drawn up by a Constituent Assembly not later than the first day of October, 1948, the present National Council shall act as the provisional administration, shall constitute the Provisional Government of the State of Israel.

THE STATE OF ISRAEL will be open to the immigration of Jews from all countries of their dispersion; will promote the development of the country for the benefit of all its inhabitants; will be based on the precepts of liberty, justice and peace taught by the Hebrew Prophets; will uphold the full social and political equality of all its citizens, without distinction of race, creed or sex; will guarantee full freedom of conscience, worship, education and culture; will safeguard the sanctity and inviolability of the shrines and Holy Places of all religions; and will dedicate itself to the principles of the Charter of the United Nations.

THE STATE OF ISRAEL will be ready to cooperate with the organs and representatives of the United Nations in the implementation of the Resolution of the Assembly of November 29, 1947, and will take steps to bring about the Economic Union over the whole of Palestine.

We appeal to the United Nations to assist the Jewish people in the building of its State and to admit Israel into the family of nations.

In the midst of wanton aggression, we yet call upon the Arab inhabitants of the State of Israel to return to the ways of peace and play their part in the development of the State, with full and equal citizenship and due representation in its bodies and institutions - provisional or permanent.

We offer peace and unity to all the neighboring states and their peoples, and invite them to cooperate with the independent Jewish nation for the common good of all.

Our call goes out to the Jewish people all over the world to rally to our side in the task of immigration and development and to stand by us in the great struggle for the fulfillment of the dream of generations - the redemption of Israel.

With trust in Almighty God, we set our hand to this Declaration, at this Session of the Provisional State Council, in the city of Tel Aviv, on this Sabbath eve, the fifth of Iyar, 5708, the fourteenth day of May, 1948."

Again, this had to happen before the coming of the Lord Jesus. Now, things to come.

1. The obvious acceleration of lawlessness
2. Increase in apostasy (abandonment of loyalty, 1Tim. 4:1-3)
3. The social element preparing for the one world Church
4. Knowledge will be increased.

5. The end time will be marked by a move for all religions and denominations to unify.

Matthew 24:33-34 states, *"...So likewise ye, when ye see all these things..."* (wars, seductions, false christs, persecutions, and the ruin of the Jewish nation)

V34. "VERILY I SAY UNTO YOU, THIS GENERATION SHALL NOT PASS, TILL ALL THESE THINGS BE FULFILLED."

How long is a generation? Some believe a generation is one hundred and twenty years, still others believe a generation is thirty-three years. I believe that the Bible is very clear on the number of years in a generation.

Psalms 90:10, "The days of our years are threescore years and ten; and if by reason of strength they be fourscore years, yet is their strength labor and sorrow; for it is soon cut off, and we fly away."

Threescore and ten is seventy years, and most believe it will all be over.

I think it noteworthy to state here that this generation of seventy years is only found in the New Testament. In the Old Testament only we find a generation of one hundred and twenty years.

Israel became a nation May 14, 1948. I believe that the generation who saw Israel be reborn are the ones to whom Jesus was referring when He spoke of "this generation." From then until May 14, 2018 is seventy years.

If seven of those years will be the time of the Tribulation, well, you do the math. The generation who will see Jerusalem destroyed may be alive today.

I said, MAY BE ALIVE TODAY. THE TRUTH IS, ONLY GOD KNOWS, AS I HAVE STATED MANY TIMES BEFORE.

I like what Mathew Henry wrote in his commentary in the King James Study Bible:

"We may build with more assurance upon the word of Christ than we can upon the pillars of heaven, or the strong foundations of the earth; for, when they shall be made to tremble and totter, and shall be no more, the word of Christ shall remain, and be in full force, power, and virtue (See 1Pe 1:24, 25). It is easier for heaven and earth to pass, than the word of Christ; so it is expressed, Luke 16:17 (Compare Isaiah 54:10). The accomplishment of these prophecies might seem to be delayed, and intervening events might seem to disagree with them, but do not think that therefore the word of Christ is fallen to the ground, for that shall never pass away: though it be not fulfilled, either in the time or in the way that we have prescribed; yet, in God's time, which is the best time, and in God's way, which is the best way, it shall certainly be fulfilled.."

Today, like never before, men are looking and praying for the coming of our Lord. As we look at today's weather patterns, strange things are happening.

CBS News recently reported that since we began keeping records we have never seen weather like we are experiencing today: famine, earthquakes, tsunamis in Asia with over two hundred and fifty thousand dead, and tornadoes like never before.

Thousands are dead because of this worldwide weather pattern. It is true that the rapture will be the most startling event of this age and dispensation.

The promised rapture, what does it mean? The word "rapture" comes from the Latin translation of the Greek word *harpazō*.

1Thessalonians 4:17 states: *"Then we which are alive and remain shall be caught up together with them in the clouds, to meet the Lord in the air: and so shall we ever be with the Lord."*

This is the only place in the New Testament that clearly refers to the rapture. Let's look at the words: "alive and remain", "be caught up", "clouds", and "ever be with the Lord."

Rapture means to "seize or to take away." In the rapture all Christians will be changed from this mortal body to be given a glorified body; one that will stand the trip.

The rapture is the hope of every born again Christian. We are to look for this sure rapture, not the Tribulation.

1Corinthians 15:51-52, "Behold, I shew you a mystery; We shall not all sleep, but we shall all be changed,

V52. In a moment, in the twinkling of an eye, at the last trump: for the trumpet shall sound, and the dead shall be raised incorruptible, and we shall be changed."

For an added blessing let's look at verse fifty-three:

"For this corruptible must put on incorruption, and this mortal must put on immortality."

Paul is writing about the rapture. This is not the seventh trumpet of Revelation 11:15 which states,

"And the seventh angel sounded; and there were great voices in heaven, saying, The kingdoms of this world are become the kingdoms of our Lord, and of his Christ; and he

shall reign for ever and ever."

This trumpet brings in the Millennial Kingdom, the one thousand year reign of Christ. In 1Corinthians 15:51-53, Paul is speaking concerning the rapture of the Church, and the trumpet of 1Thessalonians 4:16 which states:

"For the Lord himself shall descend from heaven with a shout, with the voice of the archangel, and with the trump of God: and the dead in Christ shall rise first."

The dead in Christ are the ones who died during the Church age, during our time of grace. Praise God! And then we who are left will be caught up to be with Him in the air.

Romans 8:23 gives us further insight into this truth:

"And not only they, but ourselves also, which have the firstfruits of the Spirit, even we ourselves groan within ourselves, waiting for the adoption, to wit, the redemption of our body."

The rapture refers to those who are saved, who have accepted the Lord Jesus Christ as his or her Savior, who will never see death as we know it, and those who will be absent from the body and present with the Lord.

Furthermore, 2Corinthians 5:8-9 states: *"We are confident, I say, and willing rather to be absent from the body, and to be present with the Lord.*

V9.Wherefore we labour, that, whether present or absent, we may be accepted of him."

What a wonderful day when we meet Christ face to face! We will never see the grave. We will be taken out of this life at the last trump.

Let's look once again at 1Corinthians 15:54.

"So when this corruptible shall have put on incorruption, and this mortal shall have put on immortality, then shall be brought to pass the saying that is written, DEATH IS SWALLOWED UP IN VICTORY."

As we look at the different events of the rapture, I find that there are many who confuse the rapture with the second coming of Christ. They are two separate events. The rapture will bring in the Tribulation period which will last for seven years.

Seven years after the rapture, there will be a second coming (THE WORD RAPTURE MEANS TO TAKE AWAY, OR TO REMOVE FROM) as recorded in Revelation 19:11-14.

The saints who went through the first rapture will return with Christ at his second coming.

Also, in Revelation 11:7-12 we have the TAKING AWAY INTO HEAVEN of the two witnesses. This will happen at the end of the second woe recorded in verse fourteen.

All of the things we read in 1Corinthians 15:51-55 must happen in order for us to enjoy all the wonderful things awaiting us.

V51. "Behold, I shew you a mystery; we shall not all sleep, but we shall all be changed.

V52. In a moment, in the twinkling of an eye, at the last trump: for the trumpet shall sound, and the dead shall be raised incorruptible, and we shall be changed.

V53. For this corruptible must put on incorruption, and this mortal must put on immortality.

V54. So when this corruptible shall have put on incorruption, and this mortal shall have put on immortality, then shall be brought to pass the saying that is written, DEATH IS SWALLOWED UP IN VICTORY.

V55. O DEATH, WHERE IS THY STING? O GRAVE, WHERE IS THY VICTORY?"

Let's take a moment and look at these verses. In verse fifty-one Paul reveals a mystery; the saved will not lie in the grave, only their bodies.

The dead in Christ shall rise first and shall be with the LORD. We shall be changed and will receive new bodies.

In verse fifty-two, Jesus' appearance will be powerful and with the great shout of a mighty king. The angels from heaven will be with Him. In a moment, the twinkling of an eye, the dead in Christ will rise incorruptible.

Those who are saved and still living before our Lord's coming will go with Him in the clouds (1Thess. 4:17). These changes must come about, for man's evil flesh must be changed. Flesh and blood cannot enter the kingdom of heaven. Verse fifty-three states that the corruptible must put on incorruption, the mortal must put on immortality.

Our old bodies must be changed into a new body, an immortal body. Without this new body man can never enjoy the things God has in store for him.

In verse fifty-four, death is swallowed up. Death is

considered the separation of soul and body and is not desired by most. We must understand that death will strip us from life as we know it, and then give to us a real life of joy, peace, and comfort, as well as an end to troubles.

In Genesis chapter three, Satan seemed to have had everything under control when Eve gave Adam the fruit of the tree, and later when Jesus was hung on the cross.

But Satan was defeated and Jesus was victorious when He came out of the grave.

Our robes shall be washed white by the blood of the Lamb. In verse fifty-five, death is being asked, where is your power now? You have no victory. Our body may die, but not the spirit of the child of God. Behold, we will live, never to die again. Death will be vanquished and disarmed; we forever shall be out of its reach.

Grave where is your victory? It will no longer be victorious. We are its prisoner, but God has taken its keys and will open the shackles of death, and will remove them. We will be free.

We will glory over death, for it will be vanquished. Death will be feared no longer. Once we were prisoners, but the prison doors of death were opened by God. Now death, where is thy victory?

Isaiah 25:8-9 records:

V8. "He will swallow up death in victory; and the Lord God will wipe away tears from off all faces; and the rebuke of his people shall he take away from off all the earth: for the LORD hath spoken it.

V9. And it shall be said in that day, Lo, this is our God; we have waited for him, and he will save us: this is the LORD; we have waited for him, we will be glad and rejoice in his salvation."

There are four things that the rapture will be:

1. The rapture will in the twinkling of an eye.
2. The rapture will be a time of cleaning.
3. The rapture will be a Pre-Tribulation gathering.
4. The rapture will be a time in which the dead will be changed and raised incorruptible.

Those who are alive at our Lord's coming will be caught up without dying (1Thess 4:11).

We will also see in the rapture the resurrection of the dead in Christ, and the resurrection of the living saints, characterized by the statement made by Jesus.

John 11:25-26, "... I am the resurrection, and the life: he that believeth in me, though he were dead, yet shall he live: And whosoever liveth and believeth in me shall never die. Believest thou this?"

The rapture will bring us to the Judgment Seat of Christ, known as the Bema Seat of Christ. Only Christians will be at this judgment.

2Corinthians 5:10 records: *"For we must all appear before the judgment seat of Christ; that every one may receive the things done in his body, according to that he hath done, whether it be good or bad."*

Look at the words Judgment Seat, *"for we must all appear"*, frightening isn't it? We will be standing before this great Judge of all judges, the One who died for us all, the LORD

JESUS CHRIST. We will be judged for what we have done, both good and bad.

The rapture will take the young and old alike, those who are alive and the dead in Christ, with Him into His glory.

Colossians 3:4 states: *"When Christ, who is our life, shall appear, then shall ye also appear with him in glory."*

Matthew Henry states that Christ is the principle and end of the Christian's life. And it will be His glory to have His redeemed with Him.

1Thessalonians 4:17 records: *"Then we which are alive and remain shall be caught up together with them in the clouds, to meet the Lord in the air: and so shall we ever be with the Lord."*

We have seen previous verses of Scripture relating to 1Thessalonians chapter four, but I think at this point I shall go into even more detail concerning its meaning. The appearance of our Lord will be prompt and with power.

All Christians will hear the shout of the King of Kings. We will see Him in His power, in all His authority, and the trumpet of God His Father shall usher in the great Conqueror, the great Redeemer.

In 1Corinthians 15:51, as recorded above, the mortal must put on immortality. These bodies will be made to inherit the kingdom of heaven, and then receive their crown of glory. Just think, we will be with Jesus, we will see Him and enjoy Him forever. There will be no warning before the rapture.

Luke 17:34-37, "I tell you, in that night there shall be two men in one bed; the one shall be taken, and the other shall be left.

V35. Two women shall be grinding together; the one shall be taken, and the other left.

V36. Two men shall be in the field; the one shall be taken, and the other left.

V37. And they answered and said unto him, Where, Lord? And he said unto them, Wheresoever the body is, thither will the eagles be gathered together."

When the trump of God sounds, the air will be full of spirits. There will be no grave so deep, no catacomb so covered, no pyramid so thick, and no ocean so deep that the sound of the trumpet will not reach. It will be the morning of the resurrection. His coming is sure. The trump of God will sound and the dead in Christ shall rise first.

1Corinthians 15:52, "In a moment, in the twinkling of an eye, at the last trump: for the trumpet shall sound, and the dead shall be raised incorruptible, and we shall be changed."

Your question may be: "Where will they go?"

Luke 17:37 states: *"And they answered and said unto him, Where, Lord? And he said unto them, Wheresoever the body is, thither will the eagles be gathered together."*

With the coming of our Lord, we will hear the words read in Scripture, "...caught up together with them in the clouds, to meet the Lord in the air..."

The Origin of His Coming

Now, let us examine the conditions of the first half the Tribulation period, the first forty-two months.

The antichrist will gradually take control, and will be praised by many. This will continue to progress throughout the second forty-two month period known as the "Great Tribulation".

Revelation 13:4, "And they worshipped the dragon" (Satan) *"which gave power unto the beast: and they worshipped the beast, saying, Who is like unto the beast? who is able to make war with him?"*

Through those troublesome times, the devil will have power through his antichrist. He will blaspheme God, and will show malice to all who are in the earth.

His power cannot reach into the place of God's safety, but he will show his cruelty on those who refuse to worship Him.

The antichrist will have victory over many, and will also try to stand up against the true Prince of princes as recorded in Daniel 8:25 which states:

"And through his policy also he shall cause craft to prosper in his hand; and he shall magnify himself in his heart, and by peace shall destroy many: he shall also stand up against the Prince of princes; but he shall be broken without hand."

God has His plans for the antichrist. I have heard, like many of you, the speculation concerning the different countries from which the antichrist may appear.

For the sake of understanding the chapters to come, let's examine eight kingdoms. The antichrist will come from one of these.

It has been said by some that all of these empires together would be known as the Revived Roman Empire.

I feel I would be doing you an injustice if I didn't share with you some notes found in the Scofield Study System Bible, KJV, that I feel will help us to understand more concerning many of the events of prophecy that we will see later in this book, dealing with most, if not all of the following empires.

1. The Egyptian Empire
2. The Assyrian Empire
3. The Babylonian Empire
4. The Medo-Persian Empire
5. The Grecian Empire
6. The Roman Empire of the Old Testament
7. The Revised Roman Empire (Which will surely be revived soon)
8. The Everlasting Empire

Daniel 2:44, "And in the days of these kings shall the God of heaven set up a kingdom, which shall never be destroyed: and the kingdom shall not be left to other people, but it shall break in pieces and consume all these kingdoms, and it shall stand for ever."

The Vision of the World Empires

In Daniel 2:31-40, Daniel interpreted the dream of Nebuchadnezzar where he saw a great statue which gives us a vision of the world empires. The four metals composing the statue are explained as symbolizing four empires not necessarily possessing the inhabited earth but divinely authorized to do so (Verse thirty-eight) and fulfilled in Babylon, Medo-Persia, Greece (under Alexander), and

Rome. The vision prophetically portrays the course of world empires and their destruction by Christ, who called this period "the times of the Gentiles" (Luke 21-24; also see Revelation 16:19).

The latter power is seen divided, first into two legs, fulfilled in the eastern and western Roman Empires, and then into ten toes (See Daniel 7:26 note). As a whole, Titus gains the imposing outward greatness and splendor of the Gentile world power.

The Smiting Stone, recorded in Daniel 2:34-35, destroys the Gentile world system in its final form with a sudden and irremediable blow, not by the gradual processes of conversion and assimilation. Then and not before, does the Stone become a mountain which fills the whole earth (Compare Dan 7:26-27).

Such a destruction of the Gentile monarchy system did not occur at the first advent of Christ. On the contrary, He was put to death by the sentence of an officer of the fourth empire, which was then at the zenith of its power.

After Christ's death, the western part of the Roman Empire fell in 476 AD and the eastern part in 1453, but no other world empire has superseded Rome because only four empires will precede Christ's return and rule.

In the New Testament the interposition of the Church age, between the first and second advents of Christ, is not a part of this vision.

The deadly wound is completed by the rapture of the Church (Rev. 13:3). The Gentile world power still continues, and the crushing blow is still suspended. The details of the end time are given in Daniel 7 and Revelation 13-19.

It is important to observe that one Gentile world power is to end in a sudden, catastrophic judgment (See Armageddon, Rev.16:13-16; 19:17).

Secondly, it is immediately to be followed by the kingdom of heaven. The God of heaven will not set up His kingdom until after the destruction of the Gentile world system.

Note that Gentile world dominion began and ends with a great statue, or image (Dan. 2:31; Rev. 13:14-15). The Stone which smites the statue, however, must not be identified with the Church, as some think, for the task of the Church is never said to be the destruction of the nations of the earth.

Chapter 8

THE BUILDING OF THE THIRD TEMPLE

Now I feel it is important that we stop and see just where we are now in history. Also, the next thing that is going to happen just before, or just after the Tribulation begins, will be the building of a new temple.

There are two different views concerning this and we will look at this a little deeper later in this chapter.

I feel at this point we need to look at the difference in the way of salvation in the Old and New Testament. First let's look at the Old Testament which was The Dispensation of law.

As we have already seen, in 70 AD Israel was conquered by Titus of Rome. On May 14, 1948, Israel became a nation once again. God is using this to let us know that we only have a very short time left.

Matthew 24:32 talks about the generation that is alive when Israel becomes a nation, would be the one that would see the coming of the Lord.

Psalms 90:10 tells us a generation is 70 years. Just yesterday I heard a preacher say that a generation at this time was one hundred years.

Not true. A generation during the Millennial Reign of Christ will be one hundred years. Scripture tells us that a person will die at one hundred years old.

Some readers will naturally ask how we can be certain that the fig tree putting forth leaves is GOD'S PROPHETIC

SYMBOL of Israel's rebirth.

In both the Old and New Testament, the symbol of the fig tree is used exclusively for Israel (Judges 9:10; 1 Kings 4:25; Luke 13:7; John 1: 50).

It has been 61 years from May 1948 to the time of this writing. You do the math. If that generation will see Jerusalem destroyed and the Tribulation is seven years, then how much time could we have left? Again no one really knows when Jesus is coming.

Now the next major road sign to His coming may be the third temple which will be built, as I said before, just before or just after the beginning of the Tribulation. I can find no one who has the answer for sure. Let's start by looking at the first temple.

The first temple was built by Solomon, King of Israel in 1000 BC. It was destroyed by the Babylonians in 586 BC.

The second temple was built by the Jews after their return to Jerusalem in 536 BC following the Babylonian captivity, and then expanded by King Herod in the first century. The ruins can be seen today.

The Jews at this time were in bondage by the Roman Empire, then scattered among all nations and returned home in 1948.

Where will the third temple be built? The temple will be rebuilt on the original sight of the Temple Mount which was first built by Solomon.

I would like to share some of what I found while reading a book by Grant R. Jefferey, a great book you should read entitled: "*The New Temple and the Second Coming.*"

Jefferey states that the temple must be built before the Tribulation. There are different thoughts concerning this. It will be just before the rapture or shortly after.

Let me close this chapter by saying this. Our LORD is the King of Kings, LORD of LORDS, and He Is God. He is the beginning and the ending. I believe the saved will be with Him in glory, we shall have all knowledge, and we will see just how much we did not know.

Forever let us give glory and honor to our Lord and Savior Jesus Christ!

Chapter 9

INTERDICTION OF THE ANTICHRIST

The antichrist speaks of peace, and at the same time will be making his plans to deceive all mankind. At the beginning of the Tribulation, Israel will make a seven year peace treaty with the antichrist, and it will receive him as predicted by Jesus in John 5:43. The following describe the antichrist:

1. He is in opposition to Christ.
2. He is a false teacher.
3. He is a man of sin.
4. He is abusive to God and man.
5. He will put great burdens on all God's people.
6. He will take complete control over all laws and ordinances, as well as religious and secular institutions. He will do this the last forty-two months of the Tribulation.

Daniel 8:23-25 lets us know that he will be broken without hands. 2Thessalonians 2:3-4 states that he is the son of perdition. He is full of destruction and wickedness, and goes about destroying both the soul and body of man (see especially verses 8-10).

Dan. 11:2-3, "And now will I shew thee the truth. Behold, there shall stand up yet three kings in Persia; and the fourth shall be far richer than they all: and by his strength through his riches he shall stir up all against the realm of Grecia.

V3. And a mighty king shall stand up, that shall rule with great dominion, and do according to his will."

And now we will look at some of the nations that will fight against God.

Dan. 11:4-9, "And when he" (the antichrist) *"shall stand up, his kingdom shall be broken, and shall be divided toward the four winds of heaven; and not to his posterity, nor according to his dominion which he ruled: for his kingdom shall be plucked up, even for others beside those.*

V5. And the king of the south shall be strong, and one of his princes; and he shall be strong above him, and have dominion; his dominion shall be a great dominion" (This is written concerning the antichrist).

V6. And in the end of years they shall join themselves together" (These nations are Egypt, Libya, Ethiopia, and Gomer. All of them will be led by Russia.); *"for the king's daughter of the south shall come to the king of the north to make an agreement: but she shall not retain the power of the arm"* (The king of the south will become weak and will lose his will to fight.); *"neither shall he stand, nor his arm: but she shall be given up, and they that brought her, and he that begat her, and he that strengthened her in these times.*

V7. But out of a branch of her roots shall one stand up in his estate, which shall come with an army, and shall enter into the fortress of the king of the north, and shall deal against them, and shall prevail." (This is referring to the antichrist who will prevail in the beginning, but will be defeated at the second coming of the Lord Jesus Christ.):

V8. "And shall also carry captives into Egypt their gods, with their princes, and with their precious vessels of silver and of gold; and he shall continue more years than the king of the north." (By this time Egypt will have turned against the antichrist and will ally with Israel.)

V9. "So the king of the south shall come into his kingdom, and shall return into his own land."

See the comments on verse six where Egypt, Libya, Ethiopia, and many believe Germany, will be defeated.

Dan.11:10-12, "But his sons shall be stirred up, and shall assemble a multitude of great forces: and one shall certainly come, and overflow, and pass through: then shall he return, and be stirred up, even to his fortress.

V11. And the king of the south shall be moved with choler, and shall come forth and fight with him, even with the king of the north: and he shall set forth a great multitude; but the multitude shall be given into his hand.

V12. And when he hath taken away" (defeated) *"the multitude, his heart shall be lifted up"* (pride); *"and he shall cast down many ten thousands: but he shall not be strengthened by it."*

The antichrist may win the battle, but he will lose the war.

Dan.11:13-15, "For the king of the north" (China, Russia, Persia, Iran, and Iraq, with other nations) *"shall return, and shall set forth a multitude greater than the former, and shall certainly come after certain years with a great army and with much riches.*

V14. And in those times there shall many stand up against the king of the south: also the robbers of thy people shall exalt themselves to establish the vision; but they shall fall.

V15. So the king of the north shall come, and cast up a mount, and take the most fenced cities: and the arms of the south shall not withstand, neither his chosen people, neither shall there be any strength to withstand."

Here the armies of the south fight against the antichrist. He is killed and Satan takes over his body.

Dan. 11:16, "But he that cometh against him shall do according to his own will, and none shall stand before him: and he shall stand in the glorious land, which by his hand shall be consumed."

Because of this combination, the antichrist will kick off this time of horror by seating himself in, and desecrating, the future temple in Jerusalem, taking all authority upon himself. He will set himself above God, and everything that is associated with a true and righteous God.

One evening I was watching the Fox news network and they were interviewing a Jewish engineer. He was asked concerning the construction of the new temple in Jerusalem and its exact location. He replied, "We are going to take down the temple of Omar and give it to them ,(the Arabs)' in pieces."

Theologians are not sure if this event will happen just before the Tribulation or just after the beginning of the Tribulation.

Matthew 24:15 records: *"When ye therefore shall see the abomination of desolation, spoken of by Daniel the prophet, stand in the holy place, (whoso readeth let him understand...)"*

In the middle of Daniel's seventieth week, the antichrist will break his covenant with Israel, stop temple worship, begin offering sacrifices that will desecrate the temple, and proclaim that he is God. The word desecrate means: to treat something sacred with disrespect.

Daniel 9:27, "And he shall confirm the covenant with many

for one week" (seven years): *"and in the midst of the week he shall cause the sacrifice and the oblation to cease, and for the overspreading of abominations he shall make it desolate, even until the consummation, and that determined shall be poured upon the desolate."*

He will cause Jewish worship to end and will set himself up as an object of worship.

2Thessalonians 2:4 states: *"Who opposeth and exalteth himself above all that is called God, or that is worshipped; so that he as God sitteth in the temple of God, showing himself that he is God."*

This act is known as the "Abomination of Desolation."

When this act takes place, the believers in Israel will flee to the mountains to a city built from solid rock, which is believed to be Petra. God will protect them there. There is a narrow opening leading into this city which cannot be easily penetrated.

Rev. 12:14, "And to the woman were given two wings of a great eagle, that she might fly into the wilderness, into her place, where she is nourished for a time, and times, and half a time" (three and one-half years), *"from the face of the serpent."*

Again, this is written concerning Israel. Now that Israel has been neutralized, the antichrist will be praised by the world.

Rev. 13:4, "And they worshipped the dragon which gave power unto the beast: and they worshipped the beast, saying, Who is like unto the beast? who is able to make war with him?"

The antichrist will destroy many people according to Daniel 8:25, *"And through his policy also he shall cause craft"* (special skills) *"to prosper in his hand; and he shall magnify himself in his heart, and by peace shall destroy many: he shall also stand up against the Prince of princes; but he shall be broken without hand."*

After the antichrist prescribes the above policy, persecution will spread upon the believers. False teachers and prophets shall come, like today, and thousands of true believers I know will be massacred, as in happening today in places like India and Africa.

Matt. 24:9, "Then shall they deliver you up to be afflicted, and shall kill you: and ye shall be hated of all nations for my name's sake."

At this point let's look at the antichrist and the real power behind him, Satan himself. I do not know of anyone who presents the antichrist better than Edward Hindson in the King James Prophecy Study Bible.

The Bible clearly portrays the coming of a world leader who will negotiate a peace treaty with Israel in the last days. The term "antichrist" appears only in

1John 2:18, "Little children, it is the last time: and as ye have heard that antichrist shall come, even now are there many antichrists; whereby we know that it is the last time."

1John 4:3, "And every spirit that confesseth not that Jesus Christ is come in the flesh is not of God: and this is that spirit of antichrist, whereof ye have heard that it should come; and even now already is it in the world."

In I John 1:7 the apostle John indicates that the antichrist of the apocalyptic era is coming in the future but he also adds that many "antichrists" (false teachers), have already come.

In the broadest sense, the spirit of antichrist is already at work in the world and has been since the beginning of time.

This spirit is the spirit of the antichrist that opposes everything that is true about Jesus Christ. However, from the very beginning of the Christian era, believers were convinced that a world leader would come on the scene who would be the embodiment of Satan.

The antichrist, indwelled by Satan, will once again identify himself when he kills the two witnesses in Jerusalem.

In Revelation chapter eleven, for forty-two months God will give power to the two witnesses, Elijah and Enoch. Some say Moses, but this can't be because Moses died.

By looking at the entire eleventh chapter of Revelation we can see why some believe this is where the Tribulation will begin. In Revelation 17:3-5 Satan is called the "Mother of Harlots", and is riding upon a beast.

Revelation 12:13, "And when the dragon saw that he was cast unto the earth, he persecuted the woman" (Israel) *"which brought forth the man child."*

Thus, the real power behind the antichrist is Satan himself. I would like to share with you some of the writing by Clarence Larkin in his book *Dispensational Truth* on the fall of Satan from heaven and his connection to the antichrist.

"As we have seen Satan still has his abode in the heavens and has access to God. But the time is coming when he shall be cast out of heaven. It is described in Rev. 12:7-17.

While Satan has been the „Accuser of the Brethren'
in all ages, the context shows that reference is here
made to the Jewish Remnant, the brethren of Christ
during the first three and one-half years of the
Tribulation period.

For Satan is cast out in the middle of the last week,
or Tribulation period. The Christians pass through
great persecution and die as martyrs. They are
referred to in Rev. 6:9-11 as the souls of them that
were slain for the „Word of God' and we are here
told (Rev.12:11) that they overcame by the „Blood
of the Lamb' and the word of their testimony „and
died as martyrs' for they loved not their lives unto
the death.

As they overcame by the Blood of the Lamb, then
the time of their overcoming must be subsequent to
the shedding of Christ's blood on Calvary, that is,
Satan, according to this account could not have
been cast out of the heaven prior to the crucifixion
of Christ.

When Jesus said: „I beheld Satan as lightning fall
from heaven.' He was not referring to some past fall
of Satan but it was a prophetic utterance, by way of
anticipation of his future fall, when he shall be cast
out of heaven by Michael the Archangel, as further
evidence as to the time of Satan's casting out.
Daniel the Prophet tells us that it will be at the time
of trouble, the Great Tribulation.

This is to come upon Daniel's people, the Jews. It is
at that time that Michael, the great Prince, is to

stand up and they shall be delivered (Daniel 12:1)."

The antichrist is known by several names and titles throughout the Bible. Each of these provides a glimpse into the many facets of his diabolical character and name. Revelation 13:1 states that one of his titles will be "The Beast":

"And I stood upon the sand of the sea, and saw a beast rise up out of the sea, having seven heads and ten horns, and upon his horns ten crowns, and upon his heads the name of blasphemy."

Note this beast rising out of the sea. This beast out of the sea is the most dominant personality to arise during the last three and one-half years of the Tribulation.

2Thessalonians 2:3 states: *"Let no man deceive you by any means: for that day shall not come, except there come a falling away first, and that man of sin be revealed, the son of perdition."*

He is also called "the wicked one" (2Thessalonians 2:8), "abomination" (Matthew 24:15; Daniel 8:23, 9:26, 11:21), and "strong-willed king" (Daniel 11:36).

The antichrist will be the most incredible human leader that the world has ever known. He will be the epitome of human genius and power and a master of deception, empowered by the father of lies, Satan himself.

Daniel 11:21 states: *"And in his estate shall stand up a vile person"* (a vile person is thoroughly bad, a contemptible person), *"to whom they shall not give the honor of the kingdom: but he shall come in peaceably, and obtain the kingdom by flatteries."*

101

At least nine factors will identify the antichrist when he comes to power:

1. He will rise to power in the last days.

Daniel 8:19-21, "And he said, Behold, I will make thee know what shall be in the last end of the indignation: for at the time appointed the end shall be.

V20. The ram which thou sawest having two horns are the kings of Media and Persia.

V21. And the rough goat is the king of Grecia: and the great horn that is between his eyes is the first king" (Nebuchadnezzar, the king of Babylon).

2. There are four kingdoms that will rule the known world: Babylon, Media-Persia, Greece, and the Roman Empire.

Daniel 8:22-23, "Now that being broken, whereas four stood up for it, four kingdoms shall stand up out of the nation, but not in his power.

V23. And in the latter time of their kingdom, when the transgressors are come to the full, a king of fierce countenance, and understanding dark sentences, shall stand up."

The fourth kingdom is Rome. In the latter days, the old Roman Empire and the fourth king are referring to the antichrist (2Thessalonians 2:3-8). It is believed that the antichrist will not want to be recognized until after the rapture.

2Thessalonians 2:3-8, "Let no man deceive you by any

means: for that day shall not come, except there come a falling away first, and that man of sin be revealed, the son of perdition" (Satan);

V4. "Who opposeth and exalteth himself above all that is called God, or that is worshipped; so that he as God sitteth in the temple of God, showing himself that he is God.

V5. Remember ye not, that, when I was yet with you, I told you these things?

V6. And now ye know what withholdeth that he might be revealed in his time.

V7. For the mystery of iniquity doth already work: only he who now letteth will let, until he be taken out of the way.

V8. And then shall that Wicked be revealed, whom the Lord shall consume with the spirit of his mouth, and shall destroy with the brightness of his coming..."

In these verses we understand that Paul is trying to help the Thessalonians of that day to understand that many things had to happen before the Lord's return, such as the interdiction of the antichrist.

Throughout the ages we have had people who were hostile to everything our Savior stands for. We all hope that civilization still has a degree of decency, but in America when over thirty-six percent of Americans say it is all right for gays to destroy the sanctity and holiness of marriage, there is something terribly wrong with our nation.

3. He will rule by international consent.

Revelation 17:12-13, "And the ten horns which thou sawest

are ten kings, which have received no kingdom as yet; but receive power as kings one hour with the beast.

V13. These have one mind, and shall give their power and strength unto the beast."

4. He will rule by deception.

Daniel 8:24, "And his power shall be mighty, but not by his own power: and he shall destroy wonderfully, and shall prosper, and practise, and shall destroy the mighty and the holy people."

5. He will be intelligent and persuasive.

Daniel 7:20, "And of the ten horns that were in his head, and of the other which came up, and before whom three fell; even of that horn that had eyes, and a mouth that spake very great things, whose look was more stout than his fellows."

6. He will control the global economy.

Revelation 13:17-18, "And that no man might buy or sell, save he that had the mark, or the name of the beast, or the number of his name.

V18. Here is wisdom. Let him that hath understanding count the number of the beast: for it is the number of a man; and his number is Six hundred three score and six."

7. He will be assisted by the false prophet.

Revelation 13:14, "And deceiveth them that dwell on the earth by the means of those miracles which he had power to do in the sight of the beast; saying to them that dwell on the earth, that they should make an image to the beast, which had the wound by a sword, and did live."

8. He will make and break a peace treaty with Israel.

Daniel 9:26-27, "And after threescore and two weeks shall Messiah be cut off, but not for himself: and the people of the prince that shall come shall destroy the city and the sanctuary; and the end thereof shall be with a flood, and unto the end of the war desolations are determined.

V27. And he shall confirm the covenant with many for one week: and in the midst of the week he shall cause the sacrifice and the oblation to cease, and for the overspreading of abominations he shall make it desolate, even until the consummation, and that determined shall be poured upon the desolate."

9. He will claim to be God.

2Thessalonians2:4, "Who opposeth and exalteth himself above all that is called God, or that is worshipped; so that he as God sitteth in the temple of God, shewing himself that he is God."

Revelation 17:12-14, "And the ten horns which thou sawest are ten kings, which have received no kingdom as yet; but receive power as kings one hour with the beast."

The ten kings are those nations which will join with the antichrist and oppose Israel and those that stand with him just before or after the rapture and at the beginning of the Tribulation.

Many today now believe the ten toed kingdom is also the ten common market countries. There is some debate concerning this.

V13. "These have one mind, and shall give their power and strength unto the beast.

V14. These shall make war with the Lamb, and the Lamb shall overcome them: for he is Lord of lords, and King of kings: and they that are with him are called, and chosen, and faithful."

There are many other details given in the Bible regarding the antichrist. Whether he will be Jewish or Gentile is not entirely clear.

However, what is clear is that he will control the last great bastion of Gentile power and will try to extend his control over the entire world. He may conquer her, but he will never control her.

Chapter 10

THE SEVEN SEALS

Before we go any further let's look at the first half of the Tribulation, the first three and one-half years. There will be:

Seven Seals

We will go through many of these seven seals later because of their significant connection to the seven trumpets and the seven vials. We then can see better the connection of the other plagues.

1. The White Horse - Cold War (Revelation 6:2)

"And I saw, and behold a white horse: and he that sat on him had a bow; and a crown was given unto him: and he went forth conquering, and to conquer."

Matthew Henry believed that the rider on the white horse was Christ. I must disagree because the second coming of Christ is recorded in Revelation 19: 11-21, which we will see in later chapters.

This is not Jesus. When our Lord comes He will have already been crowned.

2. The Red Horse - Open warfare (Revelation 6:4)

"And there went out another horse that was red: and power was given to him that sat thereon to take peace from the earth, and that they should kill one another: and there was given unto him a great sword."

3. Black Horse - Famine (Revelation 6:5)

"And when he had opened the third seal, I heard the third beast say, Come and see. And I beheld, and lo a black horse; and he that sat on him had a pair of balances in his hand."

4. Pale Horse - Death (Revelation 6:8)

"And I looked, and behold a pale horse: and his name that sat on him was Death, and Hell followed with him. And power was given unto them over the fourth part of the earth, to kill with sword, and with hunger, and with death, and with the beasts of the earth."

The rider's name is death, the king of death. After death comes hell. The thought of hell should send fear and trembling to every lost soul. Power was given to him to kill with the sword and bring hunger upon man and beast. He will bring about war, famine, and pestilence. There will be savage men, who, having divested themselves of all humanity, seek the destruction of others.

5. Martyrdom - Slain Souls (Revelation 6:9)

"And when he opened the fifth seal, I saw under the altar the souls of them that were slain for the word of God, and for the testimony which they held."

6. Great Earthquake - Lamb's Wrath (Revelation 6:12)

"And I beheld when he had opened the sixth seal, and, lo, there was a great earthquake; and the sun became black as sackcloth of hair, and the moon became as blood..."

7. Silence - Golden Censer (Revelation 8:3)

"And another angel came and stood at the altar, having a gold censer; and there was given unto him much incense, that he should offer it with the prayers of all saints upon the golden altar which was before the throne."

Seven Trumpets

1. Fire and Blood (Revelation 8:7)

"The first angel sounded, and there followed hail and fire mingled with blood, and they were cast upon the earth: and the third part of the trees was burnt up, and all green grass was burnt up."

Fire and hail mingled with blood fell upon the third part the trees and grass. Many believe this Scripture is talking about the punishment of a third of God's so called people or a country.

2. Burning Mountain (Revelation 8:8)

"And the second angel sounded, and as it were a great mountain burning with fire was cast into the sea: and the third part of the sea became blood..."

It is taught by some that Revelation eight, verse eight is talking about the burning of the city of Rome or the Roman Empire. They are talking about a totally different dispensation. The burning of Rome was hundreds of years ago. Revelation 8:8 Is referring to the future Tribulation period.

3. Star: Wormwood (Revelation 8:10)

"And the third angel sounded, and there fell a great star from heaven, burning as it were a lamp, and it fell upon the third part of the rivers, and upon the fountains of waters..."

This great star will literally fall from the heavens. Verses eleven and twelve tell us that this star is called wormwood and a third part of the waters became wormwood. Many died because of this for the waters were made bitter.

Some teach that it may be some political star or some prominent person who will corrupt the Church. How can this be, when verse ten of chapter eight tells us that this star fell like a burning lamp upon the third part of the rivers and upon the fountains of waters? No one man could do this.

4. Sun Smitten (Revelation 8:12)

"And the fourth angel sounded, and the third part of the sun was smitten, and the third part of the moon, and the third part of the stars; so as the third part of them was darkened, and the day shone not for a third part of it, and the night likewise."

5. Plague of Locusts (Revelation 9:3)

"And there came out of the smoke locusts upon the earth: and unto them was given power, as the scorpions of the earth have power."

6. Plague of Horsemen (Revelation 9:13)

"And the sixth angel sounded, and I heard a voice from the four horns of the golden altar which is before God..."

7. Christ Rules (Revelation 10:1)

"And I saw another mighty angel come down from heaven, clothed with a cloud: and a rainbow was upon his head, and his face was as it were the sun, and his feet as pillars of fire."

Seven Key Figures

1. The Woman: Israel (Revelation 12:1)

"And there appeared a great wonder in heaven; a woman clothed with the sun, and the moon under her feet, and upon her head a crown of twelve stars..."

2. The Dragon: Satan (Revelation 12:3)

"And there appeared another wonder in heaven; and behold a great red dragon, having seven heads and ten horns, and seven crowns upon his heads."

3. The Male Child: Christ (Revelation 12:5)

"And she brought forth a man child, who was to rule all nations with a rod of iron: and her child was caught up unto God, and to his throne."

4. The Remnant Saved: Israel (Revelation 12:6)

"And the woman fled into the wilderness, where she hath a place prepared of God, that they should feed her there a thousand two hundred and threescore days."

Israel will flee to Petra for three and one-half years under the shelter of God's hand until the seven years are finished.

5. The Archangel: Michael (Revelation 12:7)

"And there was war in heaven: Michael and his angels fought against the dragon; and the dragon fought and his angels..."

6. The Antichrist (Revelation 13:1)

"And I stood upon the sand of the sea, and saw a beast rise up out of the sea, having seven heads and ten horns, and upon his horns ten crowns, and upon his heads the name of blasphemy."

7. The False Prophet (Revelation 13:11)

"And I beheld another beast coming up out of the earth; and he had two horns like a lamb, and he spake as a dragon."

This false prophet arises with more power and influence to lead people astray than any before him and shall deceive the souls of men.

Now let's look at the second half of the Tribulation, three and one-half years or forty-two months, which is also known as the Great Tribulation. During this time there will be:

Seven Vials

1. Boils (Revelation 16:2)

"And the first went, and poured out his vial upon the earth; and there fell a noisome and grievous sore upon the men which had the mark of the beast, and upon them which worshipped his image."

2. Sea to Blood (Revelation 16:3)

"And the second angel poured out his vial upon the sea; and it became as the blood of a dead man: and every living soul died in the sea."

The world is full of evil, the Church will be gone, and the Holy Spirit will no longer be dealing with mankind.

3. Rivers to Blood (Revelation 16:4)

"And the third angel poured out his vial upon the rivers and fountains of waters; and they became blood."

4. Great Heat (Revelation 16:8)

"And the fourth angel poured out his vial upon the sun; and power was given unto him to scorch men with fire."

5. Darkness (Revelation 16:10)

"And the fifth angel poured out his vial upon the seat of the beast; and his kingdom was full of darkness; and they gnawed their tongues for pain."

6. Euphrates River Dried Up (Revelation 16:12)

"And the sixth angel poured out his vial upon the great river Euphrates; and the water thereof was dried up, that that the way of the kings of the east might be prepared."

7. Hail (Revelation 16:17)

"And the seventh angel poured out his vial into the air; and there came a great voice out of the temple of heaven, from the throne, saying, It is done."

Seven Dooms of Babylon

1. Devoid of Human Life (Revelation 18:4)

"And I heard another voice from heaven, saying, Come out of her, my people, that ye be not partakers of her sins, and that ye receive not of her plagues."

2. Burned with Fire (Revelation 18:8)

"Therefore shall her plagues come in one day, death, and mourning, and famine; and she shall be utterly burned with fire: for strong is the Lord God who judgeth her."

3. Destroyed in One Hour (Revelation 18:10)

"Standing afar off for the fear of her torment, saying, Alas, alas, that great city Babylon, that mighty city! for in one hour is thy judgment come."

4. People Afraid to Enter Borders (Revelation 18:11-16)

V11. "And the merchants of the earth shall weep and mourn over her; for no man buyeth their merchandise any more:

V12. The merchandise of gold, and silver, and precious stones, and of pearls, and fine linen, and purple, and silk, and scarlet, and all thyine wood, and all manner vessels of ivory, and all manner vessels of most precious wood, and of brass, and iron, and marble,

V13. And cinnamon, and odours, and ointments, and frankincense, and wine, and oil, and fine flour, and wheat, and beasts, and sheep, and horses, and chariots, and slaves, and souls of men.

V14. And the fruits that thy soul lusted after are departed from thee, and all things which were dainty and goodly are departed from thee, and thou shalt find them no more at all.

V15. The merchants of these things, which were made rich by her, shall stand afar off for the fear of her torment, weeping and wailing,

V16. And saying, Alas, alas, that great city, that was clothed in fine linen, and purple, and scarlet, and decked with gold, and precious stones, and pearls!"

5. Riches Brought to Nothing (Revelation 18:17-18)

V17. "For in one hour so great riches is come to nought. And every shipmaster, and all the company in ships, and sailors, and as many as trade by sea, stood afar off,

V18. And cried when they saw the smoke of her burning, saying, What city is like unto this great city!"

6. Violently Overthrown (Revelation 18:21)

"And a mighty angel took up a stone like a great millstone, and cast it into the sea, saying, Thus with violence shall that great city Babylon be thrown down, and shall be found no more at all."

7. Devoid of all Activity (Revelation 18:22-24)

V22. "And the voice of harpers, and musicians, and of pipers, and trumpeters, shall be heard no more at all in thee; and no craftsman, of whatsoever craft he be, shall be found any more in thee; and the sound of a millstone shall be heard no more at all in thee;

V23. And the light of a candle shall shine no more at all in thee; and the voice of the bridegroom and of the bride shall be heard no more at all in thee: for thy merchants were the great men of the earth; for by thy sorceries were all nations deceived.

V24. And in her was found the blood of prophets, and of saints, and of all that were slain upon the earth."

The Events at the Return of Christ

1. The Battle of Armageddon (Revelation19:17-19)

"And I saw an angel standing in the sun; and he cried with a loud voice, saying to all the fowls that fly in the midst of heaven, Come and gather yourselves together unto the supper of the great God;

V18. That ye may eat the flesh of kings, and the flesh of captains, and the flesh of mighty men, and the flesh of horses, and of them that sit on them, and the flesh of all men, both free and bond, both small and great.

V19. And I saw the beast, and the kings of the earth, and their armies, gathered together to make war against him that sat on the horse, and against his army."

2. Return of Christ with the Church and His Angels (Revelation 19:11-16)

V11. "And I saw heaven opened, and behold a white horse; and he that sat upon him was called Faithful and True, and in righteousness he doth judge and make war.

V12. His eyes were as a flame of fire, and on his head were many crowns; and he had a name written, that no man knew, but he himself.

V13. And he was clothed with a vesture dipped in blood: and his name is called The Word of God.

V14. And the armies which were in heaven followed him upon white horses, clothed in fine linen, white and clean.

V15. And out of his mouth goeth a sharp sword, that with it he should smite the nations: and he shall rule them with a rod of iron: and he treadeth the winepress of the fierceness and wrath of Almighty God.

V16. And he hath on his vesture and on his thigh a name written, KING OF KINGS, AND LORD OF LORDS."

3. Marriage Supper of the Lamb (Revelation 19:7)

"Let us be glad and rejoice, and give honor to him: for the marriage of the Lamb is come, and his wife hath made herself ready."

4. Antichrist and False Prophet Cast into the Lake of Fire (Revelation 19:20)

"And the beast was taken, and with him the false prophet that wrought miracles before him, with which he deceived them that had received the mark of the beast, and them that worshipped his image. These both were cast alive into a lake of fire burning with brimstone."

5. The Millennial Reign (Revelation 20:3)

"And cast him into the bottomless pit, and shut him up, and set a seal upon him, that he should deceive the nations no more, till the thousand years should be fulfilled: and after

that he must be loosed a little season."

I believe this season will be three months. There are four seasons in twelve months.

Now let's look back at the Seven Seals.

Revelation 6:17, "For the great day of his wrath" (the wrath of Jesus) *"is come; and who shall be able to stand?"*

His judgment has now come, beginning with the first six seals.

Revelation 6:2, "And I saw, and behold a white horse: and he that sat on him" (antichrist) *"had a bow; and a crown was given unto him: and he went forth conquering, and to conquer."*

The First Seal: The White Horse

The rider on the white horse will be the antichrist as stated in Revelation 6:2. *"And I saw, and behold a white horse: and he that sat on him had a bow; and a crown was given unto him: and he went forth conquering, and to conquer."*

The antichrist will be a deceiver, a liar, a destroyer, and untrustworthy. Many times in the Scriptures Satan imitated the actions of God in order to deceive.

Some teach that the man on the white horse will be Christ. I must disagree for at least three reasons:

1. The second coming of Christ is recorded in Revelation 19:11-21.

2. The antichrist will be crowned, but Rev. 19:11-12 states

that Christ is already crowned with "many crowns".

3. Read Matthew 24: 21-29. The Lord Jesus will defeat His enemies simply by the word of His mouth (Rev. 19:15, Is. 11:4, 2Thess. 2:8).

Revelation19:11-16, "And I saw heaven opened, and behold a white horse; and he that sat upon him was called Faithful and True, and in righteousness he doth judge and make war.

V12. His eyes were as a flame of fire, and on his head were many crowns; and he had a name written, that no man knew, but he himself.

V13. And he was clothed with a vesture dipped in blood: and his name is called The Word of God.

V14. And the armies which were in heaven followed him upon white horses, clothed in fine linen, white and clean.

V15. And out of his mouth goeth a sharp sword, that with it he should smite the nations: and he shall rule them with a rod of iron: and he treadeth the winepress of the fierceness and wrath of Almighty God.

V16. And he hath on his vesture and on his thigh a name written, KING OF KINGS, AND LORD OF LORDS."

Zech. 12:2-3, "Behold, I will make Jerusalem a cup of trembling unto all the people round about, when they shall be in the siege both against Judah and against Jerusalem.

V3. And in that day will I make Jerusalem a burdensome stone for all people: all that burden themselves with it shall be cut in pieces, though all the people of the earth be gathered together against it."

It is true that the Lord Jesus comes back riding on a white horse. It is told in days gone by that a man of war would not ride a white horse because it made him a target.

Our Lord will come as a conqueror and victory will be His. Also, Jesus will ride a white horse to show His power and purity. This is Christ at his second coming.

As we look at Revelation 19:11-16, we see that Jesus comes to make war, not a false peace. In Revelation 6:2, we find the antichrist, the great liar and great deceiver, come in peace but will destroy all who disagree with him.

Daniel 8:25, "And through his policy also he shall cause craft to prosper in his hand; and he shall magnify himself in his heart, and by peace shall destroy many: he shall also stand up against the Prince of princes; but he shall be broken without hand."

Now let's look back to Daniel 8:24.

"And his power shall be mighty, but not by his own power: and he shall destroy wonderfully, and shall prosper, and practise, and shall destroy the mighty and the holy people."

The Second Seal: The Red Horse, War and Bloodshed

Revelation 6:3-4, "And when he had opened the second seal, I heard the second beast say, Come and see.

V4. And there went out another horse that was red: and power was given to him that sat thereon to take peace from the earth, and that they should kill one another: and there was given unto him a great sword."

The next four seals show a sad prospect of great desolations and judgments with which God punishes those who refuse the everlasting Gospel.

The sword seen here represents armed conflict. Note that the horseman here will be given a great sword. The great sword brings war and certain death to many on the earth.

Peace on earth, which is one of mankind's greatest hopes and blessings, will be removed by war. Men who should love one another and help one another are set upon killing one another.

It is believed by some scholars that two-thirds of the world's population will be killed during the Tribulation period.

Let's look a little deeper into this conflict. Starting at Genesis 10:1, we understand how we arrived where we are now in the Scripture.

Genesis 10:1, "Now these are the generations of the sons of Noah, Shem, Ham, and Japheth."

Let's look at Japheth, the son of Noah.

Genesis 9:27, "God shall enlarge Japheth, and he shall dwell in the tents of Shem; and Canaan shall be his servant."

Japheth is the ungodly line. In Genesis 7:13 we find that Japheth and his wife were among the eight saved in the ark from the flood. He was the progenitor of many tribes inhabiting the east of Europe and the north of Asia.

Japheth was a forger of every kind of cutting instrument, and traded in vessels of brass, iron, and cassia, and some say even in slavery.

"Careful analysis of fact has concluded that there is a three-fold division of the human family (cf. Genesis 10), corresponding in a remarkable way with the great ethnological chapter of the book of Genesis.

The three great races distinguished are called the Semitic, Aryan, and Turanian (Allophylian). It cannot reasonably be questioned that the author of Genesis chapter ten has in his account the sons of Japheth classed together with the Cymry of cults such as Gomer, the Medes, Ionians or Greeks (Javan), and another one of the sons of Japheth, becoming known as the Indo-European" (*The KJV Study Bible*).

We know that Russia will be one of the main leaders in the conflict against Israel, along with many other northern nations. Let's look at them.

Ezekiel 38:5-7, "Persia" (now Iran), *"Ethiopia, and Libya with them; all of them with shield and helmet:*

V6.Gomer," (Now Germany) *"and all his bands; the house of Togarmah of the north quarters, and all his bands: and many people with thee.*

V7. Be thou prepared, and prepare for you, thou, and all thy company that are assembled unto thee, and be thou a guard unto them."

Persia, in 1935, changed its name to Iran. Ethiopia, mentioned here in verse five, is not the Ethiopia we find in Africa.

In ancient times there was an Ethiopia that bordered Persia. It is known as Cush which was located near Babylon. Libya's previous Bible name is Phut, which was located south of Russia in the general area occupied by Persia, Ethiopia, and

Gomer, which we now know as Germany.

Matthew 24:6-7, "And ye shall hear of wars and rumours of wars: see that ye be not troubled: for all these things must come to pass, but the end is not yet.

V7. For nation shall rise against nation, and kingdom against kingdom: and there shall be famines, and pestilences, and earthquakes, in divers places."

Peace will be taken from the earth. People will be talking peace, but none will be found. Famines and pestilence will indicate the beginning of great sorrows.

Jesus is telling us that a series of phenomena would characterize His return. China, Russia, India, Africa, North Korea, and many other nations can barely feed their people.

All of these nations from the north and east will come down into Israel because of its riches. The antichrist will refuse to honor his agreements with Israel, neither allow them to worship in their temple, nor allow the Palestinians to establish a state.

Zechariah 12:2-3, "Behold, I will make Jerusalem a cup of trembling unto all the people round about, when they shall be in the siege both against Judah and against Jerusalem.

V3. And in that day I will make Jerusalem a burdensome stone for all people: all that burden themselves with it shall be cut in pieces, though all the people of the earth be gathered together against it."

The Third Seal: Famine (Revelation 6:6)

"And I heard a voice in the midst of the four beasts say, A

123

measure of wheat for a penny, and three measures of barley for a penny; and see thou hurt not the oil and the wine."

The worldwide economy will collapse. We today are seeing this collapse. WE CAN SEE WITH OUR OWN EYES THIS PROPHECY BEING FULFILLED NOW IN 2010. IT WILL GET WORSE.

GAS PRICES WILL CONTINUE TO RISE. ALL OF OUR LIVING COSTS WILL JUST KEEP ON GOING UP.

We today can see the prophecy of Revelation 6:6 coming to pass.

Wheat will cost $41.80 per bushel, and barley will cost $32.50 a bushel. The angel revealed that the famine would be so severe that a daily wage will only buy enough food for one person. I have seen this kind of poverty throughout Asia and South America. We are well on our way to this kind of inflation and poverty in our own land, the USA.

Quickly, let's look at two prophecies which have been fulfilled since May 14, 1948. Israel has become a nation, and the prophecy of Revelation 6:6 has also been fulfilled, along with others. LOOK UP, OUR TIME IS AT HAND.

The Fourth Seal: The Pale Horse of Pestilence and Death

Revelation 6:8, "And I looked, and behold a pale horse: and his name that sat on him was Death, and Hell followed with him. And power was given unto them over the fourth part of the earth, to kill with sword, and with hunger, and with death, and with the beasts of the earth."

Hunger will be so widespread that even your beloved dog could turn on you. One-fourth of all mankind will perish;

over one billion people will die because of famine and war.

The three million man army, believed to be the Chinese army, along with Japan, Korea, and her allies, will also destroy many people. The horrors of this time will be greater than anything man could imagine. We will, in the pages to come, look a little closer at this great army.

The first four seals revealing the unfolding judgment of God upon the inhabitants of the earth are:

1. White: False Peace
2. Red: Warfare and Bloodshed
3. Black: Famine and Poverty
4. Pale: Disease and Death

Even though these Divine judgments are grave, the worst is yet to come.

The Fifth Seal: Souls under the Altar (Martyrs)

Revelation 6:9, "And when he had opened the fifth seal, I saw under the altar the souls of them that were slain for the word of God, and for the testimony which they held..."

John said: *"...I saw under the altar the souls of them that were slain for the word of God, and for the testimony which they held..."*

These martyrs will be with the Lord. John saw these martyrs under the altar, in the most Holy Place.

John also saw them at the feet of Jesus. All faithful martyrs, of both the Old and New Testament, along with Tribulation martyrs, are special to our Lord. They suffered and died for their beliefs without wavering through the pressures of their lives.

The Six Seal: Great Earthquake

Revelation 6:12, "And I beheld when he had opened the sixth seal, and, lo there was a great earthquake; and the sun became black as sackcloth of hair, and the moon became as blood..."

As God opens the sixth seal He unleashes an array of natural catastrophes. A massive earthquake will be the first in a series of disturbances that will show the wrath of our God during this Tribulation period.

This earthquake will not just be in just a local area. The whole earth will shake at the same time. Mountains will fall even with the ground, and rivers will overrun their banks due to wide spread flooding. Crops will be destroyed around the world and thousands will die in this great flooding, both animals and people.

The oceans will leave their banks, cities will be washed away, skyscrapers will fall on people, and thousands will drown or die by fire, or perish by other means. People will be killing each other trying to survive.

Revelation 16:18, "And there were voices, and thunders, and lightnings; and there was a great earthquake, such as was not since men were upon the earth, so mighty an earthquake, and so great."

Many believe this earthquake will be worldwide because of the phrase: *"...so mighty an earthquake, and so great".*

Joel 2:10 states: *"The earth shall quake before them; the heavens shall tremble: the sun and the moon shall be dark, and the stars shall withdraw their shining."*

Luke 21:25-26 also states: *"And there shall be signs in the sun, and in the moon, and in the stars; and upon the earth distress of nations, with perplexity; the sea and the waves roaring;*

V26. Men's hearts failing them for fear, and for looking after those things which are coming on the earth: for the powers of heaven shall be shaken."

Some believe that Luke is speaking concerning the use of powerful nuclear weapons. Could this be true?

Ezekiel 39:6 records: *"And I will send a fire on Magog, and among them that dwell carelessly in the isles: and they shall know that I am the Lord."*

It is thought that at this time God will take out His anger on the great Gog (Russia, also known as Magog). It is believed by some that Russia will launch a nuclear strike first, and that this horror will be between the United States and Europe, (excluding Germany, also known as Gomer). We will see the reason for this later.

The Seventh Seal: Silence, and the Golden Censer

Revelation 8:1, "And when he opened the seventh seal, there was silence in heaven about the space of half an hour."

After the horror of the first six "Seal Judgments" it seems that God pauses to allow men to repent from their sins, and then He appears to exact further judgments. Also, this seventh seal introduces the "Seven Trumpet Judgments."

It is believed and taught by many that the first trumpet will

127

bring in the Tribulation Period; still others say that the Tribulation doesn't start until Revelation chapter eleven with the two witnesses.

If that be so, then the Tribulation period will not have started until three and one-half years after the antichrist comes upon the scene.

Some believe Daniel chapter nine, verse twenty-seven, is where the Great Tribulation will begin with the antichrist breaking his covenant with Israel and putting an end to sacrifice and offering.

We know this as the "Abomination of Desolation", looking at the Pre-Tribulation, Pre-Millennial return of Christ.

It is believed that the antichrist will come on the scene just before the beginning of the Tribulation. However, some teach that he will come just after the Tribulation begins, and others teach he will come in the middle of the Tribulation.

I believe he will be here at the beginning of the Tribulation, and that he lives today waiting to be revealed.

The antichrist will come from the revived Grecian Empire made up of the four empires: Syria, Greece, Turkey, and Egypt. In the middle of the Tribulation six other kings will give the antichrist all of their territory and power.

Notice, January 2008, Fox News stated, "Turkey has joined the E.U. (European Union)." This old Roman Empire is complete.

Chapter 11

THE SEVEN TRUMPETS

Let's look at the seven trumpets with the corresponding Scriptures. We need to understand that the seventh seal brings on the first four trumpets (Revelation 8:1-13). Scripture tells us that with the seventh seal there was silence in heaven for one-half hour. Think of it, absolute silence.

John saw seven angels standing before God holding the seven trumpets, and he saw another angel who was holding a golden censer. In it was the incense to be offered up to God with the prayers of the saved.

Then the angel took the censer and it was thrown upon the earth. The censer was filled with fire from the altar, and there came thunder and lightning and a great earthquake. It would be good here to point out once again that the seventh seal includes all the seven trumpets. The seven trumpets include all of the seven bowls of God's wrath.

There are several reasons for the trumpets. First of all, we see that God uses seven angels to bring forth the seven judgments. Each sounding will execute judgments in order for God to show His anger upon rebellious mankind, and will also call the armies, both of God and Satan, together thus announcing His glorious return.

The First Trumpet (Rev. 8:7)

"The first angel sounded, and there followed hail and fire mingled with blood, and they were cast upon the earth: and the third part of trees was burnt up, and all green grass was burnt up."

Some teach that this fire and hail mingled with blood will come directly out of heaven; others teach that it is man's destruction upon man. My question is: Could the hail be mingled with blood if it were not a supernatural event from out of heaven?

One-third of everything will be destroyed, male and female, good and bad, rich and poor. This will also bring about a great change in the world's climate. There will be fewer trees, less oxygen, less clean water, and many people will die of hunger.

We see in the seven trumpets that Christ uses His angels in the blowing of the trumpets for the execution of God's judgment.

The Second Trumpet (Rev. 8:8-9)

"And the second angel sounded, and as it were a great mountain burning with fire was cast into the sea: and the third part of the sea became blood:

V9. And the third part of the creatures which were in the sea, and had life, died; and the third part of the ships were destroyed."

The second angel sounded his trumpet and from it there came hail and fire mingled with blood which falls upon man. A third part of every living creature will die in the sea.

Revelation 16:21 records that every hail stone that falls will weigh one talent (equal to about one hundred pounds), which causes the destruction of the food supply and a great famine because of the loss of one-third of all vegetation.

This trumpet brings about the destruction of one-third of all the ships at sea such as convoys, merchant ships, and ships of war. One-third of every living creature dies.

This is not the same judgment as the second vial found in *Rev 16:3, "And the second angel poured out his vial upon the sea; and it became as the blood of a dead man: and every living soul died in the sea."*

The second vial judgment seems to be a far worse judgment than the judgment of Revelation 8:8-9. In Revelation 16:3, every living soul died in the sea.

The Third Trumpet (Revelation 8:10-11)

"And the third angel sounded, and there fell a great star from heaven, burning as it were a lamp, and it fell upon the third part of the rivers, and upon the fountains of waters:

V11. And the name of the star is called Wormwood: and the third part of the waters became wormwood; and many men died of the waters, because they were made bitter."

The third trumpet causes a great star to fall from heaven called "wormwood", which comes from the Greek word *"absinthes"* which is described often as a bitter and poisonous herb or drug, which will pollute one-third of the fresh water on earth. What a day of horror this judgment is going to be. Thousands of people will die along with animal life and vegetation.

The Fourth Trumpet (Revelation 8:12)

"And the fourth angel sounded, and the third part of the sun was smitten, and the third part of the moon, and the third part of the stars; so as the third part of them was darkened, and the day shone not for a third part of it, and the night

likewise."

This will affect many things. One-third of the sun and moon will be smitten. This will affect the tides of the sea, the crops that feed mankind, and the rain upon the earth.

Then comes a judgment worse than the other four because of the increase of sin. Later in the seven bowls we will see even greater disasters and an increase of God's wrath.

The Fifth Trumpet (Rev. 9:1)
Note: This is also the First w Woe.

"And the fifth angel sounded, and I saw a star fall from heaven unto the earth: and to him was given the key of the bottomless pit."

The star that fell from heaven most believe was Christ, because He holds the keys to heaven and hell. Others teach that it was the fallen angels who lost their first estate, or angels from the demon world.

Revelation 9:3, "And there came out of the pit locusts upon the earth: and unto them was given power, as the scorpions of the earth have power."

The Abyss was opened and smoke rose from within, and the sky was darkened by the smoke. From out of the smoke came locusts upon the earth to torment man for five months but they cannot kill him. They have a king over them called Apollyon, the Destroyer.

They had no power over the earth; they could not hurt the earth, trees, grass or the saints of God with His name in their forehead.

Those without God's name in their foreheads will not be killed but tormented for five months. Men will seek death but cannot find it.

Many believe the locusts are a large group of demons that will plague mankind during the Tribulation. I believe that is a true interpretation.

The bottomless pit will be opened. *Revelation 9:2, "And he opened the bottomless pit; and there arose a smoke out of the pit, as the smoke of a great furnace; and the sun and the air were darkened by reason of the smoke of the pit."*

Locusts will come upon the earth. A destroyer will come, an angel out of the pit (believed to be Satan himself). His name shall be called in the Hebrew tongue, *"Abaddon",* or in the Greek tongue *"Appollyon."*

Also in the fifth trumpet, the first woe will come from the bottomless pit upon all those that are not the sealed ones of God with His mark in their foreheads for five months.

Rev 9:1, "And the fifth angel sounded, and I saw a star fall from heaven unto the earth: and to him was given the key of the bottomless pit."

NOTICE, this horror is for the ones NOT sealed with the mark of GOD in their foreheads.

Revelation 9:3-4, "And there came out of the smoke locusts upon the earth: and unto them was given power, as the scorpions of the earth have power.

V4. And it was commanded them that they should not hurt the grass of the earth, neither any green thing, neither any tree; but only those men which have not the seal of God in their foreheads."

Revelation 9:11, "And they had a king over them, which is the angel of the bottomless pit, whose name in the Hebrew tongue is Abaddon, but in the Greek tongue hath his name Apollyon."

It is very interesting that this judgment was for those without the seal of God. Those with the seal of God, I believe, will be the one hundred and forty-four thousand witnesses, along with the multitude of Gentiles who will be saved during the Tribulation through the preaching of the Word of God.

These two verses show the supernatural efforts which God will manifest during that time to bring as many as possible to Him.

Right here let me state again that if you have heard the Gospel, understood the Gospel, and then said NO to it, you will not be saved during the Tribulation (Rev. 9:20:21). God's Word tells us you will believe a lie told you by the antichrist and Satan.

The Sixth Trumpet (Revelation 9:13-21)
Note: This is also the Second Woe.

"And the sixth angel sounded, and I heard a voice from the four horns of the golden altar which is before God,

V14. Saying to the sixth angel which had the trumpet, Loose the four angels which are bound in the great river Euphrates.

V15. And the four angels were loosed, which were prepared for an hour, and a day, and a month, and a year, for to slay the third part of men.

V16. And the number of the army of the horsemen were two hundred thousand thousand: and I heard the number of them.

V17. And thus I saw the horses in the vision, and them that sat on them, having breastplates of fire, and of jacinth, and brimstone: and the heads of the horses were as the heads of lions; and out of their mouths issued fire and smoke and brimstone.

V18. By these three was the third part of men killed, by the fire, and by the smoke, and by the brimstone, which issued out of their mouths.

V19. For their power is in their mouth, and in their tails: for their tails were like unto serpents, and had heads, and with them they do hurt.

V20. And the rest of the men which were not killed by these plagues yet repented not of the works of their hands, that they should not worship devils, and idols of gold, and silver, and brass, and stone, and of wood: which neither can see, nor hear, nor walk:

V21. Neither repented they of their murders, nor of their sorceries, nor of their fornication, nor of their thefts. "

Much will happen during the sixth trumpet and the Second Woe leading up to the final trumpet. One third of all mankind will die.

The Tribulation population will be reduced by more than one-half.

Now at this point, let's look at some of the events that will bring all of this about.

135

According to Daniel 11:39-45, the king of the south, or Egypt, will move against Israel, and the king of the north, Russia, will follow her.

Some state that because of the history of Gomer (Germany), he will come down and attack Israel, but also Egypt, Libya, Ethiopia, and Africa. Many believe this invading nation will be led by Russia.

Note, you hear nothing about the United States of America at this time. Some think it could have been destroyed. I do not believe so; however, I believe America has lost its leading role in the world because she will turn from God.

In the year 2009, our nation has lost the respect of the world. Our dollar is worth less today than any time in history. America, the most powerful nation on earth, has been made weak by godless people who lust after their own power; a nation led by the people, no longer led by the people, but men and women who seek after their own lust. Yes, America could have easily lost its leadership in this world.

I believe at this point we should try and pinpoint the whereabouts of the antichrist. At this time the antichrist will be the head of the old Roman Empire with his headquarters in Jerusalem.

The Seventh Trumpet (Rev. 11:15)

"And the seventh angel sounded; and there were great voices in heaven, saying, The kingdoms of this world are become the kingdoms of our Lord, and of his Christ; and he shall reign for ever and ever."

Mankind could have repented, but would not. Man has

hardened his heart.

This trumpet will bring in the beginning of the Millennial Reign of Christ. The kingdoms of this world will be totally destroyed by this coming of Christ, and sin as we know it will be vanquished.

Revelation 16:21, "And there fell upon men a great hail out of heaven, every stone about the weight of a talent: and men blasphemed God because of the plague of the hail; for the plague thereof was exceeding great."

(The weight of a talent is about one hundred pounds. That is a big chunk of ice.) We can't imagine the horror of hail falling at that size, homes being destroyed, cars, trains, buses, thousands of people being crushed, vast areas totally destroyed.

This world is almost ready for the second coming of Christ. His coming will happen during the seventh bowl judgment.

At this time the unsaved will be blasphemed and cannot be saved. The seventh vial is also the last of the seven plagues, and completes the seven trumpets and the seven seals.

Note the following quote from the K.J.V. Prophecy Study Bible:

"The seventh trumpet sounds, though other significant events must still unfold. John records that the angels rejoice because the count down to Christ's absolute victory over Satan has begun."

The twenty-four elders fell upon their faces in worship of God, acknowledging that His glorious majestic reign is about to be fulfilled at the Second Coming of Christ.

Chapter 12

THE SEVEN VIALS OF GOD'S WRATH

Before we go into the Seven Bowls, there are seven figures I would like you to see in order for us to understand the terms that will be used later.

1. The Woman: Israel

Revelation 12:1 "And there appeared a great wonder in heaven; a woman clothed with the sun, and the moon under her feet, and upon her head a crown of twelve stars..."

The woman represents the faithful Jews who are waiting for the coming of Christ. The crown of stars represents the twelve tribes of Israel.

2. The Dragon: Satan
Note: This is also the Third Woe

Revelation 12:3-4, "And there appeared another wonder in heaven; and behold a great red dragon, having seven heads and ten horns, and seven crowns upon his heads.

V4. And his tail drew the third part of the stars of heaven, and did cast them to the earth: and the dragon stood before the woman which was ready to be delivered, for to devour her child as soon as it was born."

Revelation 12:9, "And the great dragon was cast out, that old serpent, called the Devil, and Satan, which deceiveth the whole world: he was cast out into the earth, and his angels were cast out with him."

Satan has seven heads, ten horns, and seven crowns. This gives him power over most of the world. The Dragon stood before the woman, Israel, as she was going to bring forth her Son (Jesus).

3. The Male Child: Christ

Revelation 12:5, "And she brought forth a man child, who was to rule all nations with a rod of iron: and her child was caught up to God, and to his throne."

4. The Archangel: Michael

Revelation 12:7-9, "And there was war in heaven: Michael and his angels fought against the dragon; and the dragon fought and his angels,

V8. And prevailed not; neither was their place found any more in heaven.

V9. And the great dragon was cast out, that old serpent, called the Devil, and Satan, which deceiveth the whole world: he was cast out into the earth, and his angels were cast out with him."

5. The Remnant: Saved Israel

Revelation 12:6, "And the woman fled into the wilderness, where she hath a place prepared of God, that they should feed her there a thousand two hundred and threescore days."

Revelation 12:14, "And to the woman were given two wings of a great eagle, that she might fly into the wilderness, into her place, where she is nourished for a time, and times, and half a time, from the face of the serpent."

Hosea 2:14-15, "Therefore, behold, I will allure her, and

bring her into the wilderness, and speak comfortably unto
her.

*V15. And I will give her her vineyards from thence, and the
valley of Achor for a door of hope: and she shall sing there,
as in the days of her youth, and as in the day when she came
up out of the land of Egypt."*

6. The First Beast out of the Sea: Antichrist

*1John 2:18, "Little children, it is the last time: and as ye
have heard that antichrist shall come, even now are there
many antichrists; whereby we know that it is the last time."*

*1John 4:1-3, "Beloved, believe not every spirit, but try the
spirits whether they are of God: because many false prophets
are gone out into the world.*

*V2. Hereby know ye the Spirit of God: Every spirit that
confesseth that Jesus Christ is come in the flesh is of God:*

*V3. And every spirit that confesseth not that Jesus Christ is
come in the flesh is not of God: and this is that spirit of
antichrist, whereof ye have heard that it should come; and
even now already is it in the world."*

*Matthew24:24, "For there shall arise false Christs, and false
prophets, and shall shew great signs and wonders; insomuch
that, if it were possible, they shall deceive the very elect."*

7. The Second Beast out of the Earth: False Prophet

*Rev. 13:11-15, "And I beheld another beast coming
up out of the earth; and he had two horns like a lamb, and he
spake as a dragon.*

V12. And he exerciseth all the power of the first beast before him, and causeth the earth and them which dwell therein to worship the first beast, whose deadly wound was healed.

V13. And he doeth great wonders, so that he maketh fire come down from heaven on the earth in the sight of men,

V14. And deceiveth them that dwell on the earth by the means of those miracles which he had power to do in the sight of the beast; saying to them that dwell on the earth, that they should make an image to the beast, which had the wound by a sword, and did live.

V15. And he had power to give life unto the image of the beast, that the image of the beast should both speak, and cause that as many as would not worship the image of the beast should be killed."

The antichrist seems to do well but will go about to destroy God's people. This beast is a counterfeit of the Holy Spirit.

Revelation 16:1-2 records:

"And I heard a great voice out of the temple saying to the seven angels, Go your ways, and pour out the vials of the wrath of God upon the earth.

V2. And the first went, and poured out his vial upon the earth; and there fell a noisome and grievous sore upon the men which had the mark of the beast, and upon them which worshipped his image."

Verse one possibly reveals the final seven and the most severe judgments of the great Tribulation, which is a period consisting of three and one-half years. These judgments will prepare the world for the final coming of our LORD and

GOD, JESUS CHRIST.

Vial One:

Revelation 16:2, "And the first went, and poured out his vial upon the earth; and there fell a noisome and grievous sore upon the men which had the mark of the beast, and upon them which worshipped his image."

This verse reveals the first vial that is poured out which affects only those with the mark of the beast. It is a plague like unto the plague of Egypt found in Exodus 8:12. These Egyptian plagues were not poured out at the same time. They were seven different events.

Our Lord has His plan and nothing will be done outside His will, such as the water turning to blood, boils, sores, and earthquakes. We shall also see the fall of the antichrist and the destruction of all he commanded.

The verse also reveals a "noisome" (offensive), "grievous" (oppressive) sore causing much grief and sorrow. Those who will receive the "mark of the beast" have marked themselves with sin.

As stated in the King James Study Bible: "The vials of God's wrath fulfill the punishment of the lost during the Tribulation period." In Revelation 16:1-12 John describes the last seven vial judgments. During the final days of the Tribulation the Christian will be persecuted.

Vial Two:

Revelation 16:3, "And the second angel poured out his vial upon the sea; and it became as the blood of a dead man; and every living soul died in the sea."

This vial judgment parallels the second trumpet of Revelation 8:8-9, and the Egyptian plague of Exodus 7: 20-21.

Vial Three:

Revelation 16:4, "And the third angel poured out his vial upon the rivers and fountains of waters; and they became blood."

Notice this verse again. The vial was poured on the rivers and fountains of unsalted water, and all water became blood. At this time all fish and every marine animal died.

No pure drinking water could be found upon the earth. This plague parallels the third trumpet of Revelation chapter eight, verses ten and eleven.

Vial Four:

Revelation 16: 8-9, "And the fourth angel poured out his vial upon the sun; and power was given unto him to scorch men with fire.

V9. And men were scorched with great heat, and blasphemed the name of God, which hath power over these plagues: and they repented not to give him glory."

By this time men have become so hardened against God and everything decent that they are beyond reach. It is a heart-breaking time in which they live. Men are going to and fro seeking after the things of this world, their hearts cold to God, and beyond the reach of God's truths.

Vial Five:

Revelation 16:10-11, "And the fifth angel poured out his vial upon the seat of the beast; and his kingdom was full of darkness; and they gnawed their tongues for pain,

V11. And blasphemed the God of heaven because of their pains and their sores, and repented not of their deeds."

This fifth vial brings darkness upon the beast and his kingdom. He has set up his throne, either in Rome or Jerusalem. (I believe it will be in Jerusalem, however, some believe that it will be in Rome.) It doesn't matter where, but what does matter is that he will set up his throne. His people will suffer pain, agony, and fear.

Vial Six:

Revelation 16:12, "And the sixth angel poured out his vial upon the great river Euphrates; and the water thereof was dried up, that the way of the kings of the east might be prepared."

With the river Euphrates dried up the armies of Gog will invade Israel. China, along with many other eastern countries, will come down upon God's people.

Vial Seven:

Revelation 16:17-21, "And the seventh angel poured out his vial into the air; and there came a great voice out of the temple of heaven, from the throne, saying, It is done.

V18. And there were voices, and thunders, and lightnings;

and there was a great earthquake, such as was not since men were upon the earth, so mighty an earthquake, and so great.

V19. And the great city was divided into three parts, and the cities of the nations fell: and great Babylon came in remembrance before God, to give unto her the cup of the wine of the fierceness of his wrath.

V20. And every island fled away, and the mountains were not found.

V21. And there fell upon men a great hail out of heaven, every stone about the weight of a talent: and men blasphemed God because of the plague of the hail; for the plague thereof was exceeding great."

As the armies of the world gather to fight God's army, the Lord will send thunder, lightning, and great earthquakes like never before seen by mankind. Great hail will fall from the sky: stones weighing a hundred pounds.

Again, man will curse God because of these plagues. Now the seven vials and the last seven plagues of Revelation chapter fifteen, verses six through eight complete the seven trumpets and the seven vials.

Now let's look at some of the plagues.

Revelation 16:18, "And there were voices, and thunders, and lightnings; and there was a great earthquake, such as was not since men were upon the earth, so mighty an earthquake, and so great."

In this verse we read of an earthquake so great that cities around the world will be destroyed and thousands will be killed.

146

Islands will sink to the ocean bottom. Large mountains will be distorted to the point that they will not be found. Large hail stones weighing one hundred pounds each will fall from the sky.

Men will be killed, and houses will be destroyed by the great weight of the hail.

Daniel 12:1, "And at that time shall Michael stand up, the great prince which standeth for the children of thy people: and there shall be a time of trouble, such as never was since there was a nation even to that same time: and at that time thy people shall be delivered, every one that shall be found written in the book."

Isaiah 26:20-21, "Come, my people, enter thou into thy chambers, and shut thy doors about thee: hide thyself as it were for a little moment, until the indignation be overpast."

This is likened to the Passover in Egypt. Not one person with the mark of God will even be touched by this hail that will, by the anger of God, will fall upon the unjust.

V.21 "For, behold, the LORD cometh out of his place to punish the inhabitants of the earth for their iniquity: the earth also shall disclose her blood, and shall no more cover her slain."

The majority of Bible history will have been fulfilled by this time; some believe at least four-fifths. The seven vials continue with voices, thundering, great lightning, and a great earthquake at the sounding of the seventh trumpet. After this there will be a great storm.

This confirms that the seven seals include the trumpet and

vial judgments, and the end of the seventieth week of Daniel 9:24. In other words, the opening of the seventh seal reveals events that are about to happen.

The blast of the trumpet announces the events of the vial judgments as forthcoming. The outpouring of the seventh vial executes the events as stated.

Now, before we look into the second advent of the Messiah, we need to study the two witnesses and the Battle of Armageddon.

Please Note: My studies on these subjects came from the KJV Prophecy Study Bible, the Matthew Henry Study Bible (KJV), and Scofield Study Bible (KJV), along with the Open Bible.

Chapter 13

THE TWO WITNESSES

It is taught that the "two witnesses" will appear during the sixth trumpet. God will send these two witnesses to judge the most important matters of their day.

Revelation 11:3, "And I will give power unto my two witnesses, and they shall prophesy a thousand two hundred and threescore days, clothed in sackcloth."

There are three and one-half years, based on the formula of three hundred and sixty-four and one-fourth days in a year, in which these two men will have the power from God to destroy His enemies with fire from heaven.

At the end of the first three and one-half years of the Tribulation, these two men will be killed by the antichrist. Who are the two witnesses?

Elijah and Enoch are the two witnesses, and are men of God who have not died. Some teach that Moses will be one of the witnesses, but that can't be because he died and was buried by God in the mountain overlooking the Promised Land.

Deuteronomy 34:5-6 states:

"V5. So Moses the servant of the LORD died there in the land of Moab, according to the word of the LORD.

V6. And he buried him in a valley in the land of Moab, over against Beth-peor: but no man knoweth of his sepulchre unto this day."

Still, others argue that some died and have come back to life, which is true. Elijah and Enoch were the only two men who went to heaven without dying, and they will come back, for they must die (Heb. 9:27). 2Kings 2:11 records the translation of Elijah.

2Kings 2:11, "And it came to pass, as they still went on, and talked, that, behold, there appeared a chariot of fire, and horses of fire, and parted them both asunder; and Elijah went up by a whirlwind into heaven."

Now let's look at Enoch:

Genesis 5:24, "And Enoch walked with God: and he was not; for God took him."

Hebrews 11:5, "By faith Enoch was translated that he should not see death; and was not found, because God had translated him: for before his translation he had this testimony, that he pleased God."

Please remember, all men must die, and after this the judgment.

Hebrews 9:27, "And as it is appointed unto men once to die, but after this the judgment."

I have read some writers who say, "I know what the Bible has to say in Hebrews chapter nine, verse twenty-seven, but what about those who will go up in the rapture?" No problem. You can't change the meaning of God's Word. The Word teaches us that we will be changed in the twinkling of an eye (1Cor. 15:51-52).

During this twinkle we will drop off the old man (the flesh), and will be made like the highest God. Think about this, even our Lord Jesus Christ had to die, but only once, in order to be the sacrifice for our sins. Consider this: If Moses was one of the two witnesses that had to die twice, which man, Elijah or Enoch would spend eternity with God without dying? This cannot be. It is appointed unto man to die just one time, then the judgment.

Chapter 14

THE BATTLE OF ARMAGEDDON

When did the fighting first begin between the Arabs and the Jews, and when will it end?

In response to this question, the fight started with the sons of Abraham, Isaac and Ishmael.

This fight will continue until the end of the first three and one-half years of the Tribulation when nearly all of the Arab nations, with Russia as their ally, will gather together against Israel.

This is the second battle in the Middle East. Russia will attack Israel after the antichrist shatters his peace agreement with the Jews.

Daniel 9:27, "And he shall confirm the covenant with many for one week: and in the midst of the week he shall cause the sacrifice and the oblation to cease, and for the overspreading of abominations he shall make it desolate, even until the consummation, and that determined shall be poured upon the desolate" (Also see Ezekiel 38:15-16).

Along with the ten kings from the west, kings from the east, China, will march against Israel (Da. 7:24; Rev. 13:1). Also, kings from the south (Da. 11:44), with most of Africa (Da. 11:11), will invade Israel.

Daniel 7:24, "And the ten horns out of this kingdom are ten kings that shall arise: and another shall arise after them; and he shall be diverse from the first, and he shall subdue three kings."

Revelation 13:1, "And I stood upon the sand of the sea, and saw a beast rise up out of the sea, having seven heads and ten horns, and upon his horns ten crowns, and upon his heads the name of blasphemy."

Daniel 11:44, "But tidings out of the east and out of the north shall trouble him: therefore he shall go forth with great fury to destroy, and utterly to make away many."

Daniel 11:11, "And the king of the south shall be moved with choler, and shall come forth and fight with him, even with the king of the north: and he shall set forth a great multitude: but the multitude shall be given into his hand."

These invading armies will meet the armies of the LORD to battle, and they will be destroyed by the very one they rejected (Joel 3:9-14; Psalms 2:2, 3; Rev. 19:11-21). This will be the bloodiest battle in world history (Rev. 9:16) and will be the closing battle in the Middle East.

Revelation 9:16, "And the number of the army of the horsemen were two hundred thousand thousand: and I heard the number of them."

So many will die that for two hundred miles the blood will be so deep it will reach to the horse's bridle and it will take seven months to bury the dead (Rev. 14:20; Ezk. 39:12).

Ezekiel 39:12, "And seven months shall the house of Israel be burying of them, that they may cleanse the land."

In my studies of this battle, I find that most are basically teaching the same thing, maybe with some slight differences, but most are in agreement concerning the location of the battle, the armies involved, and the authority of the Scriptures. But, there is some misunderstanding concerning the battle of Armageddon and the battle of Gog and Magog.

We will look at more concerning this later.

In studying for this book, I have read many books by men I respect, and who have proven their knowledge of the Scriptures.

It is through these Godly men, the King James 1611 translation, and with the direction of the Holy Spirit we all must seek the truth.

One of the great men of our lifetime, in my opinion, was Brother Oliver B. Greene. I have everything that he had written before his death in my library. A few books were published after he went home to be with the Lord. I would like to share with you just a few of his thoughts at this point concerning these two battles. Brother Greene states:

"The time of these two battles is not the same. The battle of Gog, recorded in Ezekiel chapter thirty-nine, is during the Great Tribulation, before the millennium.

The battle of Gog, recorded in Revelation chapter twenty, verse eight, is at the close of the millennium, and is a least one thousand years later after the first battle.

1. In Ezekiel, Gog comes down from the North Country.

2. In Revelation, Gog is made up of people of all nations.

3. In Ezekiel, Gog is the prince, the ruler of Magog, Russia.

4. In Revelation, Gog is the devil himself.

5. In Ezekiel, Gog is against Israel.

6. In Revelation, Gog fights against God.

7. In Ezekiel, Gog is destroyed with a sword.

It takes seven months to bury the dead. The armies of Gog in Revelation, which number so many soldiers that the numbers are as the sands of the seas, will be destroyed with fire from God out of heaven, and there will be no dead bodies to bury.

God will destroy millions before they have a chance to attack. Thus, by comparing Scripture to Scripture, we see these two battles could not possibly be the same.

In Joel 2:1-10, we are told of the great army from the north sweeping down upon Israel; but in chapter three, verse two, the army is made up of all nations."

Today people are choosing sides. We know many of the nations that will fight against God, but who are those that will fight the antichrist? The expositors tell us that the people of Sheba are the Arabian tribes in the south of Arabia, and that the people of Dedan are of the same blood.

These peoples, some expositors declare, are the people of Africa.

Another question asked is: "Who is Tarshish?" Many believe it is Great Britain, a nation with many colonies that could easily be called her "young lions"; nations such as America, Australia, Canada, New Zealand, and the English colonies in Africa.

I think at this time it would be good to look back to chapter three concerning the good and evil generation starting with

Noah after the flood.

Who are they? Where did they come from, and where are they going concerning Bible prophecy?

This question has been asked often, "Did Ezekiel foresee Russia coming against the Middle East and could his prophecy be true in this modern age we are living?"

I feel in order for us to truly understand, we must at times look back to some territory we have already covered, such as the Godly and ungodly generation found in chapter three.

Now let's look again at Gog and Magog, and where they belong in past Biblical history and future events.

In Russia you will find two cities, Tubal and Meshech. Then there is Togarmah and Gomer. Where did these names come from? Again we need to once again look back to chapter three of this book. But for now let's just look back to the sons of Noah after the flood.

There was Noah and his sons, Shem, Ham, and Japheth. Then look at the ungodly line, Japheth the father, and his sons, Gomer, Magog, Madai, Javan, Tubal, Meshech, and Tiras (Gen 10:1-2).

Now for a look at more of Japheth's descendants. From Magog are descended the ancient Scythians whose descendants predominate modern Russia.

Tubal and his descendants populated south of the Black Sea, then they went north and south.

Meshech, Tubal, Magog, and other nations will be included in the final battle called the Battle of God and Magog.

According to other writers I have read, in the oriental tongue, the name of the Caucasus Mountains that run through Russia means "Fort of Gog" or "Gog's last stand." The Russians call the heights of the Caucasus Mountains the Gogh.

Do we at this time see enough proof that Russia is the land of Gog and Magog?

Let's look at Ezekiel 38:1-6.

V1. "And the word of the LORD came unto me, saying,

V2. Son of man, set thy face against Gog, the land of Magog, the chief prince of Meshech and Tubal, and prophesy against him,

V3. And say, Thus saith the Lord GOD; Behold I am against thee, O Gog, the chief prince of Meshech and Tubal:

V4. And I will turn thee back, and put hooks into thy jaws, and I will bring thee forth, and all thine army, horses and horsemen, all of them clothed with all sorts of armour, even a great company with bucklers and shields, all of them handling swords:

V5. Persia, Ethiopia, and Libya with them; all of them with shield and helmet:

V6. Gomer, and all his bands; the house of Togarmah of the north quarters, and all his bands: and many people with thee."

Could it be that even more proof is needed that this battle of Gog and Magog will end all battles?

Let's see Revelation 20: 7-10.

V7. "And when the thousand years are expired, Satan shall be loosed out of his prison,

V8. And shall go out to deceive the nations which are in the four quarters of the earth, Gog and Magog, to gather them together to battle: the number of whom is as the sand of the sea.

V9. And they went up on the breadth of the earth, and compassed the camp of the saints about, and the beloved city: and fire came down from God out of heaven, and devoured them.

V10. And the devil that deceived them was cast into the lake of fire and brimstone, where the beast and the false prophet are, and shall be tormented day and night for ever and ever."

Please note that much of what I am writing comes from the Scofield Reference Bible.

Now let's take a few minutes to look back at the antichrist. Will he rule the whole earth? There are some who believe that the antichrist will rule the entire world excluding North America, South America, Canada, and other lands which were not known at that time. I don't believe America, Canada, Great Britain, New Zealand, and Australia will turn against Israel at first.

They all will later during the battle of Armageddon for just a season. Then many also teach that some nations will also turn against the antichrist. We know that Egypt will repent and fight with Israel.

In the last three and one-half years of the Tribulation many nations will turn against the armies of the antichrist. His kingdom will be set up in Jerusalem, and there will be a war like never before seen on the face of the earth.

The nations that fight against the antichrist will be led by ten European nations. He takes Jerusalem as his capital, and afterwards he stands in its temple proclaiming himself to be God (2Thess. 2:3-4; Dan. 11:45).

The weakened northern army of Russia and her allies, believed to be Egypt, will rebel against the antichrist. At this time his attention will go toward the invading armies of the north and east.

Daniel 11:44 records: *"But tidings out of the east and out of the north shall trouble him: therefore he shall go forth with great fury to destroy, and utterly to make away many."*

Israel will flee into the mountains, safe for the moment.

Matthew 24:16-17, "Then let them which be in Judaea flee into the mountains:

V17. Let him which is on the housetop not come down to take any thing out of his house…"

There are some who compare Matthew chapter 24 with Luke 21:20-24. Luke wrote concerning the destruction of Jerusalem which was fulfilled by Titus in A.D. 70.

Luke 21:20-24, "And when ye shall see Jerusalem compassed with armies, then know that the desolation thereof is nigh.

V21. Then let them that are in Judaea flee to the mountains; and let them which are in the midst of it depart out; and let not them that are in the countries enter thereinto.

V22. For these be the days of vengeance, that all things which are written may be fulfilled.

V23. But woe unto them that are with child, and to them that give suck, in those days! for there shall be great distress in the land, and wrath upon this people.

V24. And they shall fall by the edge of the sword, and shall be led away captive into all nations: and Jerusalem shall be trodden down of the Gentiles, until the times of the Gentiles be fulfilled."

Matthew wrote of the crisis in Jerusalem after the antichrist makes his claim to be God, which is called an abomination in Rev. 19:20.

Rev. 19:20, "And the beast was taken, and with him the false prophet that wrought miracles before him, with which he deceived them that had received the mark of the beast, and them that worshipped his image. These both were cast alive into a lake of fire burning with brimstone."

There is no question concerning the nations that will march against Israel. They are Africa, Libya, Russia, Gomer, and some believe Egypt, along with many other nations.

However, there are others who believe that Egypt will not be among those nations that march against Israel. My question for them is, what about Daniel 11:42 which states:

"He shall stretch forth his hand also upon the countries: and the land of Egypt shall not escape."

Isaiah chapter nineteen records that Egypt will be won to Christ. The Matthew Henry Study Bible (KJV) notes state that Egypt and Assyria will become partners in serving God, and Israel will make a third part with them.

Though Egypt was formerly a house of bondage, and Assyria an unjust invader, all this shall be forgiven and forgotten. They are all like His people whom He takes under His protection.

The King James Study Bible notes on Isaiah 19:21-25 state that the prophet Isaiah saw a day when Egypt would be converted to the knowledge of the Lord. They further state that Christ Himself will rule over Egypt during the Millennial Kingdom. Please note that when the statement "in that day" is written in these verses it is referring to the Millennial Kingdom.

The Application Study Bible (KJV) notes on Isaiah state: "After Egypt's chastening it will turn from idols and worship God. This prophecy will come true „in that day,' the future day of Christ's rule. Christ will not rule until the Millennial."

So Egypt very well could be a part of the nations that will come against Israel.

The term, in that day, is used many times in a reference to the day of the Lord. This is the day that God either does something to fulfill His purpose, or to perform His purpose. According to *Matthew Henry's Commentary on the Whole Bible,* the phrase "The day of the Lord" is found or referred to 5,658 times in Scripture and "day of the Lord" is found or referred to 3,773 times.

Zechariah 2:11, "And many nations shall be joined to the

LORD in that day..."

This is the day of the LORD.

Isaiah 51: 6, "Lift up your eyes to the heavens and look upon the earth beneath: for the heavens shall vanish away like smoke, and the earth shall wax old like a garment, and they that dwell therein shall die in like manner: but my salvation shall be for ever, and my righteousness shall not be abolished."

Isaiah is writing about in the day of the Lord.

1Corinthians 3:13, "Every man's work shall be made manifest: for the day shall declare it, because it shall be revealed by fire; and the fire shall try every man's work of what sort it is."

Paul is writing about the day of the Lord; the day of His judgment.

2Peter 3:10, "But the day of the Lord will come as a thief in the night; in the which the heavens shall pass away with a great noise, and the elements shall melt with fervent heat, the earth also and the works that are therein shall be burned up."

Now back to the nations. Isaiah 16:1-4, 2Kings 14:7, Isaiah 42:11, and Isaiah 7:1 state that Moab, Edom, and Ammon, what we now know as Jordan, will aid the Jews. Most of the Jews will go into the city of Petra which is protected by a narrow passage of rock clefts.

Daniel 11:40-45 teaches us that Edom, Moab, and Amman had escaped had escaped the conquest of the antichrist by this time.

The Location of the Battle of Armageddon

Armageddon is the Greek term for the area of Palestine located along the southern rim of the plain of Esdraelon known alternately as the valley of Jezreel. This great battlefield was the crossroads of two ancient trade routes, and the sight of major victories as well as disasters and sudden great misfortune for the Israelites (See Judges 4:15; 1Samuel 31:8; 2Kings 23:29-30).

To the Jews Armageddon became synonymous with terrible and final destruction. This battle will take place at the end of the Tribulation. It will occur in various locations, but will be centered in this area of Palestine.

The Scripture teaches us in Joel 3:2, *"I will also gather all nations, and will bring them down into the valley of Jehoshaphat, and will plead with them there for my people and for my heritage Israel, whom they have scattered among the nations, and parted my land."*

Today Israel has lost most of its land and is surrounded by people who hate her and want to destroy her. It is also believed that Jerusalem herself will be the center of the conflict. Could this be true or is it a false doctrine?

Remember, as we study this wonderful book of Revelation it is not what we think it means that counts, it is what is written that counts.

Let's look at the Scripture.

Zechariah 14:2, "For I will gather all nations against

Jerusalem to battle" (Remember, many will be coming to fight against the antichrist, and only one-half of the city will be brought into captivity); *"and the city shall be taken, and the houses rifled, and the women ravished; and half of the city shall go forth into captivity, and the residue of the people shall not be cut off from the city"* (Also, please read Zechariah 12:2-11).

At this time in the Tribulation the antichrist will command almost all the armies of the west including the nation of Israel.

Daniel 9:27 "And he shall confirm the covenant with many for one week: and in the midst of the week he shall cause the sacrifice and the oblation" (meaning a religious offering) *"to cease, and for the overspreading of abominations he shall make it desolate, even until the consummation, and that determined shall be poured upon the desolate."*

The antichrist will consolidate his military position by conquering and occupying Libya and Ethiopia, thereby controlling all of the Middle East and Northern Africa. He will center his military forces in Israel because of its strategic military and economic location.

Daniel 11:41-42, "He shall enter also into the glorious land, and many countries shall be overthrown: but these shall escape out of his hand, even Edom, and Moab, and the chief of the children of Ammon.

V42. He shall stretch forth his hand also upon the countries: and the land of Egypt shall not escape."

The other major army involved in this battle will be the army from the east.

Revelation 16:12, "And the sixth angel poured out his vial upon the great river Euphrates; and the water thereof was dried up, that the way of the kings of the east might be prepared."

The sixth angel's vial dries up the great river Euphrates, which was the eastern limit of the old Roman Empire, and had served as a natural boundary between the east and west for centuries.

The drying up of this natural border clears the way for the eastern kings to join their western cohorts in the Battle of Armageddon.

The northern nations and their allies have come down to the valley of Jezreel to fight against the antichrist; but instead they will fight against Jesus. There will be a shedding of blood like this world has never seen.

Let's look at 2 Thessalonians chapter two, verse eight. Here Jesus is seen as the great victor.

"And then shall that Wicked be revealed, whom the Lord shall consume with the spirit of his mouth, and shall destroy with the brightness of his coming."

His judgment will bring horror upon those who stand against our Lord and His saints.

Isaiah 34:2-3, "For the indignation of the LORD is upon all nations, and his fury upon all their armies: he hath utterly destroyed them, he hath delivered them to the slaughter.

V3. Their slain also shall be cast out, and their stink shall come up out of their carcases, and the mountains shall be melted with their blood."

The object of God's anger at that time will point to every nation on earth. Some teach that the USA would never turn against Israel, but we will see.

Zechariah 14:2, "For I will gather all nations against Jerusalem to battle; and the city shall be taken, and the houses rifled, and the women ravished; and half of the city shall go forth into captivity, and the residue of the people shall not be cut off from the city."

God will bring these nations together against Israel in order to have all the armies on the earth gathered in one place.

Zechariah 14:3, "Then shall the LORD go forth, and fight against those nations, as when he fought in the day of battle."

Though many captives will be taken, Jesus and his armies will descend from heaven to rescue Israel from certain destruction.

In regard to Israel being rescued by Christ, let's refer to Zechariah 12:10 which records:

"And I will pour upon the house of David, and upon the inhabitants of Jerusalem, the spirit of grace and of supplications: and they shall look upon me whom they have pierced, and they shall mourn for him, as one mourneth for his only son, and shall be in bitterness for him, as one that is in bitterness for his firstborn."

Please note that Zechariah intimated that the return of Christ would cause the Mount of Olives to split in two, revealing a valley from the Dead Sea to the Mediterranean. This valley will offer a way of escape for those survivors fleeing

167

Jerusalem. God's victory over His enemies is assured. This vision parallels the prophetic vision of the following verses:

Joel 3:11, "Assemble yourselves, and come, all ye heathen, and gather yourselves together round about: thither cause thy mighty ones to come down, O LORD."

Revelation 11:14, "The second woe is past; and, behold, the third woe cometh quickly."

Zechariah 14:3, "Then shall the LORD go forth, and fight against those nations, as when he fought in the day of battle."

Revelation 19:11-14, "And I saw heaven opened, and behold a white horse; and he that sat upon him was called Faithful and True, and in righteousness he doth judge and make war.

V12. His eyes were as a flame of fire, and on his head were many crowns; and he had a name written, that no man knew, but he himself.

V13. And he was clothed with a vesture dipped in blood: and his name is called The Word of God.

V14. And the armies which were in heaven followed him upon white horses, clothed in fine linen, white and clean."

There are six things I want us to see in these last five verses.

1. The white horse here is our Lord returning in great victory.
2. The lost world will see His power.
3. He will prove that He is the only true Messiah.
4. He will fulfill the promise of His return.
5. Men will see His total sovereignty.

(The word sovereignty means supreme ruler.)

6. He will be seen as the great victor.

2Thessalonians 2:8, "And then shall that Wicked be revealed, whom the Lord shall consume with the spirit of his mouth, and shall destroy with the brightness of his coming..."

His judgment will bring horror upon those that stand against our Lord and His saints.

Isaiah 34:2, "For the indignation of the LORD is upon all nations, and his fury upon all their armies: he hath utterly destroyed them, he hath delivered them to the slaughter."

Let's also consider Isaiah 34:3. *"Their slain also shall be cast out, and their stink shall come up out of their carcases, and the mountains shall be melted with their blood."*

The object of God's anger at this point will be the world – every nation on earth.

Zechariah 14:2, "For I will gather all nations against Jerusalem to battle; and the city shall be taken, and the houses rifled, and the women ravished; and half of the city shall go forth into captivity, and the residue of the people shall not be cut off from the city."

God will bring these nations together against Israel in order to have all of the armies of the earth together in one place.

Zechariah 14:3, "Then shall the LORD go forth, and fight against those nations, as when he fought in the day of battle."

Here, I would like for us to study THE SIGNS OF THE

RETURN OF CHRIST.

Matthew 24:34, "Verily I say unto you, This generation shall not pass, till all these things be fulfilled."

The example of the fig tree reminds Jesus' followers to stay alert and observant. Just as the fig tree indicates the seasons by its foliage, so God's people can recognize the imminence of Christ's return by the fulfillment of these signs.

God tells us that He will give us a sign so that we might know the season of His return. In Matthew 24:37-38, Jesus warns us that as the days of Noah were, the season of His coming would be the same.

There will be violence on every hand. Evil will cover the earth and man will reject God's warning. Man will do just as he did before the flood, which almost destroyed all of mankind.

1Thessalonians 5:2, "For yourselves know perfectly that the day of the Lord so cometh as a thief in the night."

Paul was telling His people, WATCH FOR THE RETURN OF CHRIST.

1Thessalonians 5:4-6, "But ye, brethren, are not in darkness, that that day should overtake you as a thief.

V5. Ye are all the children of light, and the children of the day: we are not of the night, nor of darkness.

V6. Therefore let us not sleep, as do others; but let us watch and be sober."

Paul did not want the Thessalonians to set a date for our

Lord's return, but he wanted them to understand the signs of His coming. He wanted them, with joy, to know all of the signs of His coming. Like the saints of Paul's day, we need to know the signs of the coming of Christ but never try to set a date.

The Word of God gives us many signs: famine, earthquakes, plagues, signs in the heavens, lawlessness, violence, immorality, greed, selfishness, and rebellion. In June 2003 the high court of the United States ruled that men could marry men, and women could marry women.

They now have Gay Pride Day. Places like Walt Disney World have one day a year set aside for them. This is happening all over the world. AS IT WAS IN THE DAYS OF NOAH, tens of thousands of our babies are murdered every year. There is apostasy and widespread heresy in our churches. The Bible teaches us about these last days.

2Timothy 3:3-5, "Without natural affection, trucebreakers, false accusers, incontinent, fierce, despisers of those that are good,

V4. Traitors, heady, highminded, lovers of pleasures more than lovers of God;

V5. Having a form of godliness, but denying the power thereof: from such turn away."

This prophecy describes the sinful attitudes and behaviors that will be manifest in the world from the time of Paul until the last days of this age.

1. Self-Centered: This self-centered generation openly boasts of their dedication to personal pleasure rather than to God or family.

2. Covetous: A value system that honors money and possessions and elevates greed to a virtue in a corrupt and sinful society.

3. Boastful: Self promotion is emulated, boasting is widespread, and pride is no longer despised.

4. Blasphemous: These who habitually use coarse, crude, and blasphemous language are tolerated and even admired.

   Ezekiel 39:6-7, "And I will send a fire on Magog, and among them that dwell carelessly in the isles: and they shall know that I am the LORD.

   V7. So will I make my holy name known in the midst of my people Israel; and I will not let them pollute my holy name any more: and the heathen shall know that I am the LORD, the Holy One in Israel."

5. Disobedient: Widespread disobedience to parents is an accepted practice.

   Exodus 20:12, "Honour thy father and thy mother: that thy days may be long upon the land which the LORD thy God giveth thee."

6. Ungrateful and Unholy: An unprecedented lack of gratitude and a widespread contempt for righteousness pervades society.

7. Sexually Perverted: Immorality, sexual perversion, and indecency are commonplace and are readily overlooked by society.

8. Dishonest: The breakdown in personal righteousness and the loss of respect for honesty results in false accusers and contract breakers.

9. Bankrupt of Values: Loving pleasure more than loving God. A value system that appears to embrace Godly ideas, but it does not have a spiritual center. A society willing to betray itself and its beliefs for worthless pleasure or material goods.

There is apostasy and widespread heresy in the Church as described in *2 Timothy 3:5 "Having a form of godliness, but denying the power thereof: from such turn away."*

We are seeing the decay of morality throughout our land and around the world. But don't be discouraged. All of this must come to pass before our Lord's return.

There are still more signs, such as the hostility of the Arab nations toward Israel.

Ezekiel 36:12, "Yea, I will cause men to walk upon you, even my people Israel; and they shall possess thee, and thou shalt be their inheritance, and thou shalt no more henceforth bereave them of men."

ASIAN NATIONS ARE CAPABLE OF FIELDING AN ARMY OF TWO HUNDRED MILLION MEN.

Revelation 9:15-16, "And the four angels were loosed, which were prepared for an hour, and a day, and a month, and a year, for to slay the third part of men.

V16. And the number of the army of the horsemen were two hundred thousand thousand: and I heard the number of

173

them."

Luke 21:10, "Then said he unto them, Nation shall rise against nation, and kingdom against kingdom..."

Let's look at Israel and the signs of Israel.

1. The regathering of the people (Isa. 11:10-12; Ezek 37:1-12).
2. The reestablishment of the state (Zech. 12:1-6).
3. The reclamation of the land (Isa 35:1-2; Zech. 1).

Jesus Himself tells us in Luke 21:24 that we are to watch Jerusalem. When we see the city no longer under Gentile domination, then we will know that the time has come for the Lord to return.

The Second Advent of the Messiah

The Second Advent of the Messiah is the great and wonderful return of our Lord and Savior, Jesus Christ, the Lord of Lords. Let's look at a few of the characteristics of His return.

1. His return will be sudden.

Matthew 24:27, "For as the lightning cometh out of the east, and shineth even unto the west; so shall also the coming of the Son of man be."

Luke 17:24, "For as the lightning, that lighteneth out of the one part under heaven, shineth unto the other part under heaven; so shall also the Son of man be in his day."

2. His coming will be spectacular, and every eye will see Him.

Matthew 24:30, "And then shall appear the sign of the Son of man in heaven: and then shall all the tribes of the earth mourn, and they shall see the Son of man coming in the clouds of heaven with power and great glory."

These elect ones are the saints saved by their faith and trust in the Lord Jesus Christ, and nothing else.

3. His coming will be with great power.

Returning as the King of Kings, people will see the King they rejected.

Revelation 1:17, "And when I saw him, I fell at his feet as dead. And he laid his right hand upon me, saying unto me, Fear not; I am the first and the last..."

When John sees the armies of heaven which will follow Jesus into battle, these resurrected saints are clothed in white linen and riding white horses, which are symbolic of the righteousness of the saints.

Chapter 15

WILL ANYONE BE SAVED DURING THE TRIBULATION?

There are differences in thought concerning this question. Some believe that to hear the Word and not be saved is to reject the Gospel. Is this true or false?

Some will agree with what I believe, and some will not, but it really doesn't matter because this is not a cardinal doctrine. I simply mean, this has nothing to do with salvation.
Some believe and teach that if you miss the rapture and are not saved you are doomed with no chance at all.

Some teach that if you have heard the Gospel and have rejected it, you can't be saved during the Tribulation.

Some teach that if you have heard the Gospel and do not understand the Gospel, then you can be saved during the Tribulation period.

Some teach if you have heard the Gospel and are not saved then you have rejected salvation.

It is evident that a lot of good, born again, soul-winning, Christians see some things a little differently. This does not mean they are a heretic, and we need to be careful how we use that word.

Let me state once again that the only way someone will go to hell is if they are misled by Satan in believing that he or she can live for the devil, and knowingly reject the Gospel of Christ.

I would not place my eternal soul in jeopardy with the hope that I might possibly be saved during the Tribulation period.

That is a lie of Satan, and if you believe that lie you will also believe his other great lie that the antichrist is Christ.

2Thessalonians 2:10-12, "And with all deceivableness of unrighteousness in them that perish; because they received not the love of the truth, that they might be saved.

V11. And for this cause God shall send them strong delusion, that they should believe a lie:

V12. That they all might be damned who believed not the truth, but had pleasure in unrighteousness."

The view that if you have heard the Gospel and were not saved, that you cannot be saved is not necessarily true. I believe with all my soul that if a person hears the Gospel, and does not understand, when the rapture comes God will give him a chance during the Tribulation period to be saved, but not if he hears and understands the Gospel and rejects it now, before the rapture.

Matthew 13:19 records: *"When any one heareth the word of the kingdom, and understandeth it not, then cometh the wicked one"* (Satan) *"and catcheth away that which was sown in his heart. This is he which received seed by the way side."*

The phrase "catcheth away" means "to throw something away, or to waste." In order to understand we must hear with our heart.

Romans 10:10, "For with the heart man believeth unto righteousness; and with the mouth confession is made unto salvation."

Let's look deeper into this verse. People are not saved simply by confessing with the mouth, for with our mouth we testify to His saving grace, which we have believed with our hearts. The heart brings about a change of our will.

Therefore, there is no salvation without believing in your heart. If you don't understand, how can you believe unto salvation? Strong's Lexicon states: "To understand is to bring together, to put perception with the things perceived, to set or join together in mind, having the knowledge of those things which pertain to salvation." There are more than twenty-six places in Scripture that speak of understanding.

Matthew 13:13, "Therefore speak I to them in parables: because they seeing see not; and hearing they hear not, neither do they understand."

In Matthew 15:10 we are told to hear and understand.

Matthew 15:10, "And he called the multitude, and said unto them, Hear and understand..."

In Mark 8:21, the disciples saw Jesus feed the five thousand, but how is it that they didn't understand? They walked with our Lord and didn't understand. Is it that hard to believe that some hear the Gospel and don't understand?

I have heard the statement: "As a child, or young person, I went to church. I heard preaching, but I didn't really understand." Several times when soul-winning I have had people say to me, "I was brought up in another denomination, but I have never heard salvation explained that way. Now I understand." My question is, could they be saved in the Tribulation if they had not heard the truth that Jesus died for the sins of all mankind, and that they must believe in their heart that Christ rose from the dead and accept what He has done for them and receive Him as their Lord and Savior?

In Luke 2:41-50 Jesus stayed behind to talk to the wise men, and Mary and Joseph did not understand why Jesus did what He did. In Luke 18:31-34, Jesus foretold His resurrection, and verse thirty-four lets us know that they understood none of those things which were spoken.

Acts 7:25 states: *"For he supposed his brethren would have understood how that God by his hand would deliver them: but they understood not."*

Romans 3:11 states: *"There is none that understandeth, there is none that seeketh after God."*

People must have their understanding opened if they are going to be saved, AND THIS CAN ONLY BE DONE WITH THE WORD OF GOD BY THE HOLY SPIRIT.

Luke 24:45 records: *"Then opened he their understanding, that they might understand the scriptures."*

There are many more Scriptures that could be used to prove that man must understand. Lost person, if Jesus comes today and you have rejected the Gospel of our Lord Jesus Christ, you may believe that you have enough knowledge concerning the Tribulation period and the Bible that you will know the difference concerning the truth of God and the lie of the antichrist, and you will not accept him. You are wrong.

You will accept his word and be lost forever. I know I have made this statement in the above sentence, but I feel this point needs to be stressed.

Romans 10:10, "For with the heart man believeth unto righteousness; and with the mouth confession is made unto salvation."

If you cannot understand in your heart, you can't be saved. You may ask: "What about the mentally challenged?" GET REAL, God knows the heart of man.

John 16:7-9, "Nevertheless I tell you the truth; It is expedient for you that I go away: for if I go not away, the Comforter will not come unto you; but if I depart, I will send him unto you.

V8. And when he is come, he will reprove the world of sin, and of righteousness, and of judgment:

V9. Of sin, because they believe not on me..."

This means that God will put us under the convicting power of the Holy Spirit.

John 6:44 teaches us: *"No man can come to me, except the Father which hath sent me draw him: and I will raise him up at the last day."*

John 6:65 states: *"And he said, therefore said I unto you, that no man can come unto me, except it were given unto him of my Father."*

Can you be saved at will? No. Only if given by the Father. The question has been asked many times, "If during the Tribulation the Holy Spirit has been taken out, how can anyone be saved?" Please pay special attention to the phrase "except they are given by the Father" in John 6:65.

John 8:36, "If the Son therefore shall make you free, ye shall be free indeed."

John 3:36, "He that believeth on the Son hath everlasting life: and he that believeth not the Son shall not see life; but the wrath of God abideth on him."

Please notice that before the Holy Spirit was introduced, Jesus said you must believe in me.

John 15:26 states: *"But when the Comforter is come, whom I will send unto you from the Father, even the Spirit of truth, which proceedeth from the Father, he shall testify of me."*

We have God the Father, God the Son, and God the Holy Spirit; the Triune Godhead: three in one. I don't understand everything, but this is where faith comes in. I just believe it.

Chapter 16

THE FIVE CROWNS OF THE BELIEVER

During the Bema Seat Judgment, the Christian will not be able to hide anything from our Lord; His eyes see man in his nakedness. We will be unable to hide behind pretense and excuses.

1. The Crown of Righteousness

2 Timothy 4:8, "Henceforth there is laid up for me a crown of righteousness, which the Lord, the righteous judge, shall give me at that day: and not to me only, but unto all them also that love his appearing."

We are to live and work as if our Lord is coming back today. We are to live as Christ-like as possible: praying and seeking the will of our Lord in everything we do, allowing others to see God in us so that they will want what we have. The righteousness of God must shine in our lives.

2. The Crown of Glory

1Peter 5:4, "And when the chief Shepherd shall appear, ye shall receive a crown of glory that fadeth not away."

The Chief Shepherd could only be our Lord Jesus Christ. As the Chief Shepherd, He is our protector, our guide, our supplier, our judge, and He is ever-present in our time of trouble.

When the turbulence of life and the winds of destruction roar about us, when the sea of life wants to swallow us up, He, the Chief Shepherd, will always be there. He is our LORD.

3. The Crown of Life

James 1:12, "Blessed is the man that endureth temptation: for when he is tried, he shall receive the crown of life, which the Lord hath promised to them that love him."

Blessed are those who will endure, who will stand fast, who will hold on, and who will trust Christ, our Lord; he that would refuse to be swayed from the words of God. These will receive the Crown of Life.

Revelation 2:10, "Fear none of those things which thou shalt suffer: behold, the devil shall cast some of you into prison, that ye may be tried; and ye shall have tribulation ten days: be thou faithful unto death, and I will give thee a crown of life."

It is being taught by some that only those who give their life unto death will have the Crown of Life.

But they were told to endure and that it would only be for a short season. Then they would receive the Crown of Life.

This Scripture does not apply only to those people at that time, but to all believers in all times: time of law, time of grace, and the time of the Great Tribulation. If we will stand fast we will receive this Crown of Life.

4. The Crown of Rejoicing

1Thessalonians 2:19-20, "For what is our hope, or joy, or crown of rejoicing? Are not even ye in the presence of our Lord Jesus Christ at his coming?

V20. For ye are our glory and joy."

Paul's crown and joy came from the people he had won to Christ, those whose lives were changed, who were turned over to a loving Lord, and will be there at His Second Coming.

5. The Incorruptible Crown

1Corinthians 9:25, "And every man that striveth for the mastery is temperate in all things. Now they do it to obtain a corruptible crown; but we an incorruptible."

Men are striving for perfection, however, after this life the only reward they will receive is disaster if they die without Christ. But, the child of God will receive the Crown of Rejoicing. We will live with our Lord forever and forever. Amen!

The Marriage of the Lamb

Revelation 19:6-10, "And I heard as it were the voice of a great multitude, and as the voice of many waters, and as the voice of mighty thunderings, saying, Alleluia: for the Lord God omnipotent reigneth.

V7. Let us be glad and rejoice, and give honour to him: for the marriage of the Lamb is come, and his wife hath made herself ready.

V8. And to her was granted that she should be arrayed in fine linen, clean and white: for the fine linen is the righteousness of saints.

V9. And he saith unto me, Write, Blessed are they which are called unto the marriage supper of the Lamb. And he saith unto me, These are the true sayings of God.

V10. And I fell at his feet to worship him. And he said unto me, See thou do it not: I am thy fellowservant, and of thy brethren that have the testimony of Jesus: worship God: for the testimony of Jesus is the spirit of prophecy."

In Revelation chapter nineteen, verse seven, we see the glorious Marriage of the Lamb. Now the Church has been gathered together in the presence of the Great Judge, the Lord Jesus Christ.

In Revelation chapter nineteen, verse eight, the resurrected saints will receive their garments of white fine linen, the white showing the purity and righteousness of our Lord and Savior.

Revelation chapter nineteen signifies the righteousness of the saints through the atoning blood of Christ and God's sovereign grace.

This passage contains the first reference to the Church since the end of chapter three, and the seven messages to the Churches. Omitting any mention of the Church during the seven-year Tribulation reaffirms the rapture of the Church before the Tribulation period.

The Return of Christ with his Saints

Revelation 19:11-21, "And I saw heaven opened, and behold a white horse; and he that sat upon him was called Faithful and True, and in righteousness he doth judge and make war.

V12. His eyes were as a flame of fire, and on his head were many crowns; and he had a name written, that no man knew, but he himself.

V13. And he was clothed with a vesture dipped in blood: and his name is called The Word of God.

V14. And the armies which were in heaven followed him upon white horses, clothed in fine linen, white and clean.

V15. And out of his mouth goeth a sharp sword, that with it he should smite the nations: and he shall rule them with a rod of iron: and he treadeth the winepress of the fierceness and wrath of Almighty God.

V16. And he hath on his vesture and on his thigh a name written, KING OF KINGS, AND LORD OF LORDS.

V17. And I saw an angel standing in the sun; and he cried with a loud voice, saying to all the fowls that fly in the midst of heaven, Come and gather yourselves together unto the supper of the great God;

V18. That ye may eat the flesh of kings, and the flesh of captains, and the flesh of mighty men, and the flesh of horses, and of them that sit on them, and the flesh of all men, both free and bond, both small and great.

V19. And I saw the beast, and the kings of the earth, and their armies, gathered together to make war against him that sat on the horse, and against his army.

V20. And the beast was taken, and with him the false prophet that wrought miracles before him, with which he deceived them that had received the mark of the beast, and them that worshipped his image. These both were cast alive into a lake of fire burning with brimstone.

V21. And the remnant were slain with the sword of him that sat upon the horse, which sword proceeded out of his mouth:

and all the fowls were filled with their flesh."

Here John reveals the Second Coming of our Lord and Savior. The true Messiah returns in a victorious conquest with his people. Millions who have stood true to the Word of God will come back with Him.

Revelation 19:14, "And the armies which were in heaven followed him upon white horses, clothed in fine linen, white and clean."

No one will be able to stand against the army of the Lord. His Word is faithful concerning this prophecy. Please notice in verse thirteen that *"...he was clothed with a vesture dipped in blood: and His name is called The Word of God."*

I believe that the armies coming back with Christ at this time are the resurrected and raptured saints who were saved through the blood of Christ, and sat at the Marriage Supper of the Lamb.

There seems to be some misunderstanding for some people as to which coming this is. Some teach that with these verses the Second Coming, the Rapture, and the Thousand Year Reign of Christ are one, but this is not true. When the rapture comes it will be in a twinkle of an eye.

1Corinthians 15:31-55, "I protest by your rejoicing which I have in Christ Jesus our Lord, I die daily.

V32. If after the manner of men I have fought with beasts at Ephesus, what advantageth it me, if the dead rise not? let us eat and drink; for to morrow we die.

V33. Be not deceived: evil communications corrupt good manners.

V34. Awake to righteousness, and sin not; for some have not the knowledge of God: I speak this to your shame.

V35. But some man will say, How are the dead raised up? and with what body do they come?

V36. Thou fool, that which thou sowest is not quickened, except it die:

V37. And that which thou sowest, thou sowest not that body that shall be, but bare grain, it may chance of wheat, or of some other grain:

V38. But God giveth it a body as it hath pleased him, and to every seed his own body.

V39. All flesh is not the same flesh: but there is one kind of flesh of men, another flesh of beasts, another of fishes, and another of birds.

V40. There are also celestial bodies, and bodies terrestrial: but the glory of the celestial is one, and the glory of the terrestrial is another.

V41. There is one glory of the sun, and another glory of the moon, and another glory of the stars: for one star differeth from another star in glory.

V42. So also is the resurrection of the dead. It is sown in corruption; it is raised in incorruption:

V43. It is sown in dishonour; it is raised in glory: it is sown in weakness; it is raised in power:

V44. It is sown a natural body; it is raised a spiritual body. There is a natural body, and there is a spiritual body.

V45. And so it is written, The first man Adam was made a living soul; the last Adam was made a quickening spirit.

V46. Howbeit that was not first which is spiritual, but that which is natural; and afterward that which is spiritual.

V47. The first man is of the earth, earthy: the second man is the Lord from heaven.

V48. As is the earthy, such are they also that are earthy: and as is the heavenly, such are they also that are heavenly.

V49. And as we have borne the image of the earthy, we shall also bear the image of the heavenly.

V50. Now this I say, brethren, that flesh and blood cannot inherit the kingdom of God; neither doth corruption inherit incorruption.

V51. Behold, I shew you a mystery; We shall not all sleep, but we shall all be changed,

V52. In a moment, in the twinkling of an eye, at the last trump: for the trumpet shall sound, and the dead shall be raised incorruptible, and we shall be changed.

V53. For this corruptible must put on incorruption, and this mortal must put on immortality.

V54. So when this corruptible shall have put on incorruption, and this mortal shall have put on immortality, then shall be brought to pass the saying that is written, Death is swallowed up in victory.

V55. O death, where is thy sting? O grave, where is thy

victory?"

When we come to the end of 1Corinthians chapter fifteen, verses fifty-one through fifty-four, it is at this point that the dead will rise first, and we who remain will meet Him in the air. These verses clearly teach that we will meet Him in the air, and the book of The Revelation chapter nineteen, verse fourteen, teaches that next time He comes we will be with Him.

Chapter 17

THE WHITE THRONE JUDGMENT

Revelation 20:11, "And I saw a great white throne, and him that sat on it, from whose face the earth and the heaven fled away; and there was found no place for them."

There are many who believe this judgment will take place high up in the heavens, since this present universe will be dissolved.

Others teach that the judgment will take place in old Jerusalem. I am not sure where it will take place, because I would only be guessing, but I can tell you one thing for sure: it will take place.

Revelation 20:12, "...and the books were opened: and another book was opened, which is the book of life: and the dead were judged out of those things which were written in the books, according to their works."

You notice that John writes the "books", plural, not "book", singular, will be opened. The question has been asked, "Why the book of life at this judgment?" I believe it is there to show the lost that they are without excuse. This is where their name could have been.

Revelation 3:5, "He that overcometh, the same shall be clothed in white raiment; and I will not blot out his name out of the book of life, but I will confess his name before my Father, and before his angels."

You see here that John wrote: *"...I will not blot out his name out of the book of life..."*

Does this mean that your name was once in the Book of Life,

and because you did not accept Christ as your Savior, your name was taken out?

There are different thoughts concerning this. Some have taught that your name is put in the Book of Life after salvation. However, others say, no, not that it makes any difference concerning salvation.

You might be thinking right here, is this man a Calvinist? No, no, no. I am a "for whosoever will!"

John 3:16, "...whosoever believeth in him should not perish, but have everlasting life."

Note that "whosoever believeth" means anyone. I know that my name is there and can never be taken out! Praise God!

Romans 10:13, "For whosoever shall call upon the name of the Lord shall be saved."

Whosoever means one as well as the other, without exception. Therefore anyone who calls upon the Lord Jesus Christ, the Son of God, shall be saved.

As I stated in chapter one, the word saved means "to rescue from danger, or to guard from destruction."

At this judgment there shall be no acquittal; no higher court in which to appeal. If lost, you will be lost forever. There is no hope, only hell. At this judgment the dead will be judged for their evil works. The question has been asked, "Will all be punished to the same degree?"

Let's look in Luke chapter twelve, verses forty-seven through forty-eight for the answer to that question.

Luke 12:47-48, "And that servant, which knew his lord's will, and prepared not himself, neither did according to his will, shall be beaten with many stripes.

V48. But he that knew not, and did commit things worthy of stripes, shall be beaten with few stripes. For unto whomsoever much is given, of him shall be much required: and to whom men have committed much, of him they will ask the more."

We see here that it is clear some will receive more punishment than others. I believe this would be a good time to bring back to our remembrance that at the Bema Seat Judgment we will be judged the same way. We will be rewarded according to our works.

Mark 9:41 records: *"For whosoever shall give you a cup of water to drink in my name, because ye belong to Christ, verily I say unto you, he shall not lose his reward."*

Praise God. Everything we do in the name of our Lord Jesus, whether small or great, will be rewarded.

Now, let's look once more at the method of our salvation. On this subject there must not be any misunderstanding.

Therefore I will state again that we are saved through faith in the Lord Jesus Christ, as taught in the book of Ephesians, not by our own works.

Ephesians 2:8-9, "For by grace are ye saved through faith; and that not of yourselves: it is the gift of God.

V9. Not of works, lest any man should boast."

I cannot understand how anyone could teach that we are

saved through works, or that God has foreordained men to go to heaven or hell. We choose for ourselves. Why would we want to choose hell? I don't know, but many do.

Deuteronomy 32:22, "For a fire is kindled in mine anger, and shall burn unto the lowest hell, and shall consume the earth with her increase, and set on fire the foundations of the mountains."

2Samuel 22:6, "The sorrows of hell compassed me about; the snares of death prevented me..."

Psalms 9:17, "The wicked shall be turned into hell, and all the nations that forget God."

Again, we make the choice. We are separated from God because we live a disobedient life before Him. There are several reasons for our disobedience, such as:

1. Anger
2. Selfishness
3. Lasciviousness

Matt. 5:22, "But I say unto you, that whosoever is angry with his brother without a cause shall be in danger of the judgment: and whosoever shall say to his brother, Raca" (meaning an insult*), "shall be in danger of the council: but whosoever shall say, Thou fool, shall be in danger of hell fire."*

Anger is a natural thing for a person living in the flesh, but not for a Christian. To be angry without cause is sin. When you call a person a fool, it usually is said because of disgust or hatred. Because of their breaking of the law they would be in danger of the council.

What does it mean to "be in danger of the council?" It means to be punished by the Sanhedrin. The Jews had three capital punishments, each one was worse than the other. In the first punishment, they were beheaded.

In the second, they were stoned. The third punishment was that they were buried alive in the valley of the sons of Hinnon. The Greek name "Gehenna" means "a final place of eternal punishment." We are all responsible for what we do, but we all can change things in our lives.

Mark 9:43-44, "And if thy hand offend thee, cut it off: it is better for thee to enter into life maimed, than having two hands to go into hell, into the fire that never shall be quenched:

V44. Where their worm dieth not, and the fire is not quenched."

God must judge all things.

Revelation 1:18, "I am he that liveth, and was dead; and, behold, I am alive for evermore, Amen; and have the keys of hell and of death."

2Peter 2:4, "For if God spared not the angels that sinned, but cast them down to hell, and delivered them into chains of darkness, to be reserved unto judgment..."

At that time you may like to find a hiding place, but there will be no place for you to hide. The final judgment of hell will last forever.

Chapter 18

THE MILLENNIAL REIGN OF CHRIST

Revelation 20:1-4, "And I saw an angel come down from heaven, having the key of the bottomless pit and a great chain in his hand." (Praise the Lord!)

V2. "And he laid hold on the dragon, that old serpent, which is the Devil, and Satan, and bound him a thousand years,

V3. And cast him into the bottomless pit, and shut him up, and set a seal upon him, that he should deceive the nations no more, till the thousand years should be fulfilled: and after that he must be loosed a little season.

V4. And I saw thrones, and they sat upon them, and judgment was given unto them: and I saw the souls of them that were beheaded for the witness of Jesus, and for the word of God, and which had not worshipped the beast, neither his image, neither had received his mark upon their foreheads, or in their hands; and they lived and reigned with Christ a thousand years."

The mark of the Beast, the Scripture informs us, is to identify the worshippers of Satan during the Tribulation period. This will be a time of hunger and famine for the Christian. He will not be able to buy or sell without this mark (666).

When we write concerning the Millennial Reign of Christ we base it on our belief in the literal interpretation of prophecy.

I believe John is writing here of a literal one thousand year reign. These will be years of joy for the child of God.

Let's look at Isaiah 65:17-25:

V17. "For, behold, I create new heavens and a new earth: and the former shall not be remembered, nor come into mind.

V18. But be ye glad and rejoice for ever in that which I create: for, behold, I create Jerusalem a rejoicing, and her people a joy.

V19.And I will rejoice in Jerusalem, and joy in my people: and the voice of weeping shall be no more heard in her, nor the voice of crying." (This is believed by most to be the time of the Millennial Reign of Christ.)

V20. "There shall be no more thence an infant of days, nor an old man that hath not filled his days: for the child shall die an hundred years old; but the sinner being an hundred years old shall be accursed.

V21.And they shall build houses, and inhabit them; and they shall plant vineyards, and eat the fruit of them.

V22. They shall not build, and another inhabit; they shall not plant, and another eat: for as the days of a tree are the days of my people, and mine elect shall long enjoy the work of their hands.

V23. They shall not labour in vain, nor bring forth for trouble; for they are the seed of the blessed of the LORD, and their offspring with them.

V24.And it shall come to pass, that before they call, I will answer; and while they are yet speaking, I will hear.

V25. The wolf and the lamb shall feed together, and the lion shall eat straw like the bullock: and dust shall be the serpent's meat. They shall not hurt nor destroy in all my holy mountain, saith the LORD."

According to verse seventeen, there will be a new heaven and a new earth. This is not the new heaven and earth of Revelation twenty-one. According to verse twenty, those who refuse Christ will die at one hundred years of age. Please understand that he is speaking concerning the time of the one thousand year reign.

In the New Jerusalem our house will be built without hands. The grace of our wonderful Lord and Savior Jesus Christ is so great that even the people who are born during this rule can be saved, and many will be saved.

It is hard to understand how people who have seen His great love and experienced it could ever turn against our Lord. But they will as soon as Satan is released. We will see this in the pages to follow.

From the time our God put man in the garden, mankind has rejected God's plan for their lives. When Adam partook of the fruit it was because he wanted to be as God.

Genesis 3:5 states: *"For God doth know that in the day ye eat thereof, then your eyes shall be opened, and ye shall be as gods, knowing good and evil."*

Just as Adam and Eve thought they would see good and evil, we the Church need to anoint our eyes with eye salve so we might see our true condition (Rev. 3:18).

Rev.3:18, "I counsel thee to buy of me gold tried in the fire, that thou mayest be rich; and white raiment, that thou mayest be clothed, and that the shame of thy nakedness do not appear; and anoint thine eyes with eyesalve, that thou mayest see."

Let's look at this Scripture to understand its meaning concerning this Church at Laodicea. We are now in the Laodicean Church age, the last Church age before the Tribulation.

Jesus told the Laodiceans to buy their gold from Him (real spiritual treasures). Our Lord also told them to buy white garments from Him (His righteousness).

The weakness of the Church will not prevent God from keeping His promise; His kingdom will be on earth and will be ruled by the Messiah: Jesus Himself.

Laodicea prided itself on its eye salve that had healing power. God told them that He was the healing they needed so they could see the truth.

John 9:39, "And Jesus said, For judgment I am come into this world, that they which see not might see; and that they which see might be made blind."

Christ was showing them that our value comes from Him, not the wealth of this world. Again, we are in the Laodicean time. We are no different from them. We want possessions and achievements, but all these things are valueless compared to God's everlasting kingdom.

God would discipline this lukewarm Church, just as He is doing to us right now, unless we turn from our indifference toward Him. Are we a lukewarm Church?

This church was complacent, rich, and self-satisfied, but without Christ.

He knocked at the door of their hearts, but they were busy enjoying worldly things. Material possessions satisfy only for a short period. Sounds just like us, doesn't it?

When Christ comes He will physically descend to earth and stand on the Mount of Olives. There will be an earthquake, and the mountain will split from the Mediterranean to the Mount of Olives, opposite to the Temple Mount, and then south to the Dead Sea.

Then, according to Ezekiel 43:2-5, Jesus will enter Jerusalem through the Eastern Gate. This gate has been sealed shut and no one other than the King of Kings shall enter in.

Ezekiel 44:2, *"Then said the Lord unto me; This gate shall be shut, it shall not be opened, and no man shall enter in by it; because the LORD, the God of Israel, hath entered in by it, therefore it shall be shut."*

This gate has been closed for many centuries, and was sealed by the Muslims when they rebuilt the walls of Jerusalem in 825 A.D., over twelve hundred years ago.

A Muslim graveyard now occupies the area where one enters through the Eastern Gate going to the temple. The Muslims put the cemetery there to ensure that no holy man would walk through, as an attempt to thwart the fulfillment of Ezekiel's prophecy.

Now the importance of the Millennial Reign is simply to point out the beginning of the eternal kingdom of our LORD GOD. This is seen several times in Revelation twenty.

In Revelation chapter twenty, verse ten we read of the end of Satan's rule.

Rev. 20:10, "And the devil that deceived them was cast into the lake of fire and brimstone, where the beast and the false prophet are, and shall be tormented day and night for ever and ever."

Please remember that this will happen after the battle of Gog and Magog, not before the battle of Armageddon.

Thank God for Revelation 21:1 which states: *"And I saw a new heaven and a new earth..."*

Praise God, all things are made new. The righteousness and justice of God will be restored, all sin will be dealt with, and He will rule the earth with a rod of iron.

Revelation 12:5 records: *"And she brought forth a man child, who was to rule all nations with a rod of iron: and her child was caught up unto God, and to his throne."*

But even in this great time of plenty people will rebel against God, led by Satan himself.

Revelation 20:3, "And cast him" (Satan) *"into the bottomless pit, and shut him up, and set a seal upon him, that he should deceive the nations no more, till the thousand years should be fulfilled: and after that he must be loosed a little season."*

Verse seven through verse nine states:

V7. "And when the thousand years are expired, Satan shall be loosed out of his prison,

V8. And shall go out to deceive the nations which are in the four quarters of the earth, Gog and Magog, to gather them together to battle: the number of whom is as the sand of the sea.

V9. And they went up on the breadth of the earth, and compassed the camp of the saints about, and the beloved city: and fire came down from God out of heaven, and devoured them."

The reference here in verse eight to Gog and Magog is similar to that of Ezekiel chapter thirty-eight. Also notice that only Gog and Magog are mentioned in verse eight. The Scripture does not name the other nations, such as Gomer, Iran, China, and others.

The battle of Gog and Magog and the battle of Armageddon are two separate battles. One of the greatest blessings that will come from the Millennial Kingdom is that the curse which came because of Adam and Eve will end.

Corruption will be a thing of the past, and we will live in His righteousness. The curse that was upon the earth will be lifted, and instead of thorns there will be roses.

Isaiah 35:1, "The wilderness and the solitary place shall be glad for them; and the desert shall rejoice, and blossom as the rose."

Isaiah 33:24, "And the inhabitant shall not say, I am sick: the people that dwell therein shall be forgiven their iniquity."

Isaiah 29:17, "Is it not yet a very little while, and Lebanon shall be turned into a fruitful field, and the fruitful field shall be esteemed as a forest?"

Just think, the badlands of Lebanon made like a great forest, with waterfalls, running streams, lakes and rivers; and all of this because the curse upon the earth was lifted. Sin has been conquered.

The covenant made with Abraham will be realized in the Millennial Kingdom, and the promise of peace made to Israel will be consummated.

Chapter 19

THE MARRIAGE SUPPER OF THE LAMB

The marriage union of man and woman appears repeatedly in Scripture in the Old Testament. Unrepentant Israel was likened to an adulterous wife (Hosea 2: 1-8). In ancient Israel there were three phases to a legal marriage:

1. The first phase was the betrothal; this was a legally binding agreement entered into by both parties.

2. The second phase involved the coming of the bridegroom to meet his bride.

3. The third phase was the celebration and the marriage supper.

How does this relate to the coming of Christ? Our spiritual life echoes this marriage ritual:

1. Our spiritual betrothal with Christ began with our salvation.

2. The rapture of the Church is equivalent to the bridegroom coming for the bride.

3. Once the bride has been collected, there will be a great marriage feast celebration between Christ and the completed bride.

The question being put forth by many is, "When will this wedding occur?" To me the Scripture suggests that the Marriage Supper of the Lamb must take place sometime between the rapture of the Church and the coming of Christ back to earth with His saints at the Battle of Armageddon.

Revelation 19:7 states: *"Let us be glad and rejoice, and give honour to him: for the marriage of the Lamb is come, and his wife hath made herself ready."*

These two are different events. John affirms this sequence of events in Revelation 19:7 with two separate statements:

"...the marriage of the Lamb is come, and his wife" (the bride) *"hath made herself ready."*

The Greek word translated "come" is written in the aorist tense, signifying an act that was completed in the past, and needs no other action or limitation. This indicates that the marriage will be already consummated by this point, and it will precede the Second Coming of Christ, also known as the Second Advent.

Only after describing the marriage supper does John then record his vision of Christ's return to earth at the battle of Armageddon.

One question that has often been asked is, "If the whole Church is the bride, then who are the guests invited to the wedding?"

John chapter three, verse twenty-nine states: *"He that hath the bride is the bridegroom: but the friend of the bridegroom, which standeth and heareth him, rejoiceth greatly because of the bridegroom's voice: this my joy therefore is fulfilled."*

Who are the friends written about here? They can only be the Tribulation saints who will die a martyr's death, along with the Old Testament saints and the host of heaven.

The Old Testament saints are not the body of Christ.

Remember what John recorded in chapter three, verse twenty-nine, *"...because of the bridegroom's voice: my joy therefore is fulfilled."* John was a guest at the wedding.

John's detailed vision of the marriage supper includes a description of the bride's garments. She is dressed in fine linen, clean and white.

Revelation 19:8, "And to her was granted that she should be arrayed in fine linen, clean and white: for the fine linen is the righteousness of saints."

The Church is also seen as completely cleansed through the atonement of Christ. It is not by any work we could have done. We are purified solely by Christ's righteousness applied to our hearts through faith in Him as our Lord and Savior.

The bride, being clothed in fine linen, affirms that the Church has already participated in the Bema Seat Judgment where rewards are given for faithful works.

Romans 14:10, "But why dost thou judge thy brother? or why dost thou set at nought thy brother? for we shall all stand before the judgment seat of Christ" (See also 2Cor. 5:10).

Revelation 19:14, "And the armies which were in heaven followed him upon white horses, clothed in fine linen, white and clean."

Now let's look at the events we have seen thus far before we look at the five crowns and rewards. We have studied:

1. The Church Age
2. The Rapture of the Church

3. The Bema Seat of Christ
4. The Battle of Armageddon
5. The Marriage Supper of the Lamb
6. The Return of Christ to Earth

Let's look further into the judgment of the saints. Many teach that at the Bema Seat Judgment of Christ we will not be judged for our sins, but for our works, whether good or bad. God's grace determines what the Christian receives for his obedience to Christ and the position of service he will have during the Kingdom of God.

Paul summarizes the concept of God's grace in the Scripture.

Those who will be saved during the Tribulation will go to be with Christ in our Father's house.

1Thessalonians 4:17-18, "Then we which are alive and remain shall be caught up together with them in the clouds, to meet the Lord in the air: and so shall we ever be with the Lord.

V18. Wherefore comfort one another with these words."

If we suffer with Him, we shall also reign with Him.

Revelation 2:26-27, "And he that overcometh, and keepeth my works unto the end, to him will I give power over the nations:

V27. And he shall rule them with a rod of iron; as the vessels of a potter shall they be broken to shivers: even as I received of my Father."

If we deny Him, He will also deny us.

Matthew 10:32-33, "Whosoever therefore shall confess me before men, him will I confess also before my Father which is in heaven.

V33. But whosoever shall deny me before men, him will I also deny before my Father which is in heaven."

If we are faithless, He remains faithful.

2Timothy 2:11-13, "It is a faithful saying: For if we be dead with him, we shall also live with him:

V12. If we suffer, we shall also reign with him: if we deny him, he also will deny us:

V13. If we believe not, yet he abideth faithful: he cannot deny himself."

1Corinthians 4:2-5, "Moreover it is required in stewards, that a man is found faithful.

V3. But with me it is a very small thing that I should be judged of you, or of man's judgment: yea, I judge not mine own self.

V4. For I know nothing by myself; yet am I not hereby justified: but he that judgeth me is the Lord.

V5. Therefore judge nothing before the time, until the Lord come, who both will bring to light the hidden things of darkness, and will make manifest the counsels of the hearts: and then shall every man have praise of God."

One of the heartbreaks I have seen in my many years of ministry is people judging people. Lives are destroyed by basing a judgment on a half-truth, an all out lie, or just a misunderstanding.

We need not judge others. Judging is the responsibility only of our Lord because nothing can be hid from Him.

Luke 12:2-3, "For there is nothing covered, that shall not be revealed; neither hid, that shall not be known.

V3. Therefore whatsoever ye have spoken in darkness shall be heard in the light; and that which ye have spoken in the ear in closets shall be proclaimed upon the housetops."

We need to take heed to what is being said here. It would stop a lot of sin, especially the sin of gossip.

Hebrews 4:13, "Neither is there any creature that is not manifest in his sight: but all things are naked and opened unto the eyes of him with whom we have to do."

We shall hide nothing from the eyes of God.

2Corinthians 5:10, "For we must all appear before the judgment seat of Christ; that every one may receive the things done in his body, according to that he hath done, whether it be good or bad."

Here Paul is speaking concerning the saved. If we as Christians, pastors, evangelists, missionaries, and Church members would stop judging one another, and just judge ourselves, we would not have time to judge others. OUR LORD will judge the saints.

Psalms 103:12, "As far as the east is from the west, so far hath he removed our transgressions from us."

Because of his saving grace, God has put our sins as far as

the east is from the west, not to be looked upon for evermore. All of this is because of His grace. As Christians, why can't we do the same?

Now the sins we commit after salvation, will we answer for them? Some say no. They believe that we have been saved from our past and future sins.

Hell is not in the picture for us, and we are being judged for our works here on earth.

It is sure that we will lose many of our rewards after salvation because of our sins.

2 Corinthians 5:10 states: *"For we must all appear before the judgment seat of Christ; that every one may receive the things done in his body, according to that he hath done, whether it be good or bad."*

Of course, I'm sure that most people would like to think that there would be no judgment for sins after salvation. After all, we have that old man to deal with day after day.

Like most of you I have heard this many times. But nothing we can say can change the truth: we shall all be judged according to what we have done in this body.

Hebrews 4:13, "Neither is there any creature that is not manifest in his sight: but all things are naked and opened unto the eyes of him with whom we have to do."

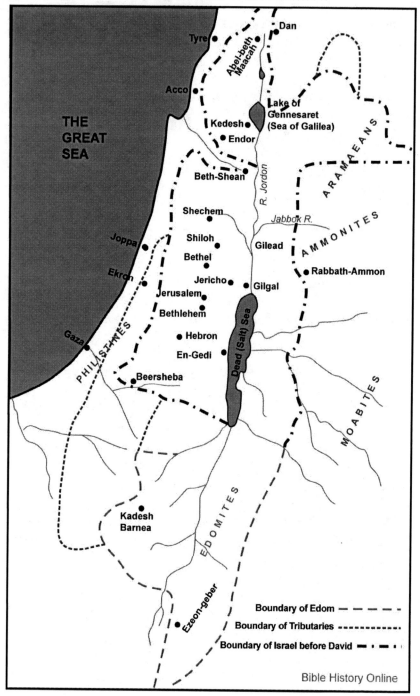

Chapter 20

THE BOUNDARIES OF THE TRIBES OF ISRAEL DURING THE MILLENNIAL REIGN OF CHRIST

There have been many questions asked concerning the Millennial Kingdom and who will be living at that time alongside of the twelve tribes of Israel. Who are they? Where will they come from, and in what area will they be living?

In this chapter we are going to explore God's Word for these answers.

Ephesians 4:4-6, "There is one body, and one Spirit, even as ye are called in one hope of your calling;

V5. One Lord, one faith, one baptism,

V6. One God and Father of all, who is above all, and through all, and in you all."

Verse four begins with the statement, "There is one body..." Paul is emphasizing the unity of all believers; that Jews and Gentiles are equal in Christ.

Gentiles could become Christians without having to conform to Jewish traditions. However, many Jewish Christians who had always been prejudiced against the Gentiles thought they were not true believers.

Paul thought that they should view the Gentiles as their brothers in Christ, on an equal level. God is the Father of all mankind who believe, in all cultures and races.

Ephesians 3:6, "That the Gentiles should be fellowheirs, and of the same body, and partakers of his promise in Christ by the gospel."

Ephesians 2:14, "For he is our peace, who hath made both one, and hath broken down the middle wall of partition between us..."

Let's see where each tribe of Israel will be living and also who the strangers are that live among them. The following page will explain.

Now let's look at Isaiah 11:10-12.

V10. "And in that day there shall be a root of Jesse, which shall stand for an ensign of the people; to it shall the Gentiles seek: and his rest shall be glorious."

The statement made in Isaiah 11:10 explains itself. The root of Jesse has been seen by some as the grandfather root of Christ, because Jesse was the Father of David. God's Word teaches that Jesus is the offspring of David, or Jesus the root from David, the ensign.

An ensign is a sign such as a flag that will pinpoint a tribe of people and will identify which tribe it is, such as the tribe of Judah, the house of Jacob, and so on through the twelve tribes. This is just like the USA which has a flag for each of the fifty states.

V11. "And it shall come to pass in that day, that the Lord shall set his hand again the second time to recover the remnant of his people, which shall be left, from Assyria, and from Egypt, and from Pathros, and from Cush, and from Elam, and from Shinar, and from Hamath, and from the islands of the sea.

V12. And he shall set up an ensign for the nations, and shall

216

assemble the outcasts of Israel, and gather together the dispersed of Judah from the four corners of the earth."

Now let's look at the boundaries of their inheritance, starting with Ezekiel 47:13 through verse 23.

V13. "Thus saith the Lord GOD; This shall be the border, whereby ye shall inherit the land according to the twelve tribes of Israel: Joseph shall have two portions.

V14. And ye shall inherit it, one as well as another: concerning the which I lifted up mine hand to give it unto your fathers: and this land shall fall unto you for inheritance.

V15. And this shall be the border of the land toward the north side, from the great sea, the way of Hethlon, as men go to Zedad;

V16. Hamath, Berothah, Sibraim, which is between the border of Damascus and the border of Hamath; Hazar-hatticon, which is by the coast of Hauran.

V17. And the border from the sea shall be Hazar-enan, the border of Damascus, and the north northward, and the border of Hamath. And this is the north side.

V18. And the east side ye shall measure from Hauran, and from Damascus, and from Gilead, and from the land of Israel by Jordan, from the border unto the east sea. And this is the east side.

V19. And the south side southward, from Tamar even to the waters of strife in Kadesh, the river to the great sea. And this is the south side southward.

217

V20. The west side also shall be the great sea from the border, till a man come over against Hamath. This is the west side.

V21. So shall ye divide this land unto you according to the tribes of Israel.

V22. And it shall come to pass, that ye shall divide it by lot for an inheritance unto you, and to the strangers that sojourn among you, which shall beget children among you: and they shall be unto you as born in the country among the children of Israel; they shall have inheritance with you among the tribes of Israel.

V23. And it shall come to pass, that in what tribe the stranger sojourneth, there shall ye give him his inheritance, saith the Lord GOD."

Who are the strangers? They are the Gentiles that are saved during the Tribulation period and have passed over into the millennial age, according to Ezekiel 47:22-23. Again let's read.

V22. "And it shall come to pass, that ye shall divide it by lot for an inheritance unto you, and to the strangers that sojourn among you"

(THIS MEANS THAT THE SAVED TRIBULATION GENTILES WILL LIVE AMONG THE TWELVE TRIBES OF ISRAEL.)

"which shall beget children among you: and they shall be unto you as born in the country among the children of Israel; they shall have inheritance with you among the tribes of Israel."

NOW LET'S LOOK AT VERSE TWENTY THREE.

V23. "And it shall come to pass, that in what tribe the stranger sojourneth, there shall ye give him his inheritance, saith the Lord GOD."

Many times we must repeat Scripture in order to express the importance of a particular subject.

In these Scriptures we will find that Ezekiel is describing ways of worship, in order to have some diversity in worship. There will be no sacrifice because the Lamb has already been killed (JESUS CHRIST).

Thank God this sacrifice did not stay dead. He arose, He arose, praise God, He arose.

In Chapter 47:1-12, this river is similar to the river mentioned in Revelation 22:1.

Revelation 22:1, "And he shewed me a pure river of water of life, clear as crystal, proceeding out of the throne of God and of the Lamb."

Genesis 2:10, "And a river went out of Eden to water the garden; and from thence it was parted, and became into four heads."

The river symbolized life from God and the blessings that flow from His throne. It is a gentle, safe, deep river, expanding as it flows.

The sea that will heal refers to the Dead Sea, a body of water so salty that nothing can live in it. This river will heal the Dead Sea waters so they can support life. This is another picture of the life giving nature of water that flows from

God's temple.

You should read the whole chapter of Ezekiel chapter forty-eight.

Let's look a little closer at this chapter.

Revelation 7:5 states: *"Of the tribe of Juda were sealed twelve thousand. Of the tribe of Reuben were sealed twelve thousand. Of the tribe of Gad were sealed twelve thousand."*

This intimates likewise that all are subjects of Christ's Kingdom who have obtained faith in Christ, Jews and Gentiles alike, all saved and partakers of Christ.

The strangers who sojourn among them will have families and have an inheritance among the tribes of Israel.

This could not have happened during the time of Joshua's day, but will happen in the latter day. This act is a general naturalization (to confer citizenship on), which will teach the Jews who is their neighbor, not only of their own nation and religion, but those who wanted to be their friends. They will in the latter days invite those strangers to come in among them to serve their God.

God was instructing the Jews to accept the strangers who joined themselves to Him even though they were not of the seed of Abraham.

The Tribulation saints might question, "Why is it that the son of strangers can be accepted when at the time of Joshua that would never have happened?"

What a Gospel revival it will be when the partition wall between Jews and Gentiles will be taken down and both will be as one in the eyes of God, and the Gentiles will at that time receive the same blessing as Israel.

Isaiah 56:3, "Neither let the son of the stranger, that hath joined himself to the LORD, speak, saying, The LORD hath utterly separated me from his people: neither let the eunuch say, Behold, I am a dry tree."

The Gentiles were aliens from the covenant of promise, and feared they would be separated by the Jews. They were not as one of them, because they were not of the seed of Abraham. Like the eunuchs, they said, "I am a dry tree."

Then another question is asked, "Where will the bride of Christ staying during the one thousand year reign of Christ?"

Wherever Jesus is, there we will be also. Most believe the New Testament saints will live in Jerusalem with Christ as He rules with His saints. He tells us His bride, wherever He is, we shall be there also, forever with the LORD.

Let's look at Revelation 7:15-17.

V15. "Therefore are they before the throne of God, and serve him day and night in his temple: and he that sitteth on the throne shall dwell among them.

V16. They shall hunger no more, neither thirst any more; neither shall the sun light on them, nor any heat.

V17. For the Lamb which is in the midst of throne shall feed them, and shall lead them unto living fountains of waters: and God shall wipe away all tears from their eyes."

As previously stated, these are those who went through the Tribulation period without taking the mark of the beast. God said that they would serve Him day and night. It is believed by many that the Tribulation saints will also serve the bride of Christ.

We know that after the one thousand year reign of Christ, the devil will be put in hell forever, the earth is destroyed by fire, and then there will be a new heaven and a new earth.

Where will the Bride of Christ and the Tribulation saints live after the millennial? There are two different views.

The Tribulation saints and the Old Testament saints saved under the law are believed by many to live on the earth.

Revelation 21:24-26, "And the nations of them which are saved shall walk in the light of it: and the kings of the earth do bring their glory and honour into it.

V25. And the gates of it shall not be shut at all by day: for there shall be no night there."

Notice, the kings of the EARTH will bring their glory and honor into it. Into it means it is coming from the outside. The earth will bring their glory and honor into it.

V26. "And they shall bring the glory and honour of the nations into it."

It is thought by some that the Old Testament saints will plant vineyards and build houses.

Some teach that only the bride will be in the new city of Jerusalem and that only the bride will live in the houses made without hands and walk on the streets of gold.

I have read where it has been taught that God would come

down to earth to worship with man, and man will go to the new city to worship with the Father.

Revelation 21:3, "And I heard a great voice out of heaven saying, Behold, the tabernacle of God is with men, and he will dwell with them, and they shall be his people, and God himself shall be with them, and be their God."

Some teach that the bride is the twelve tribes of Israel and the born again Gentiles.

Let's look at Revelation 21:9-14.

V9. "And there came unto me one of the seven angels which had the seven vials full of the seven last plagues, and talked with me, saying, Come hither, I will show thee the bride, the Lamb's wife.

V10. And he carried me away in the spirit to a great and high mountain, and shewed me that great city, the holy Jerusalem, descending out of heaven from God,

V11. Having the glory of God: and her light was like unto a stone most precious, even like a jasper stone, clear as crystal;

V12. And had a wall great and high, and had twelve gates, and at the gates twelve angels, and names written thereon, which are the names of the twelve tribes of the children of Israel:

V13. On the east three gates; on the north three gates; on the south three gates; and on the west three gates.

V14. And the wall of the city had twelve foundations, and in them the names of the twelve apostles of the Lamb."

Remember, at the rapture Jesus will be coming for His bride. The wedding feast will happen before the Second Advent and the Millennial Reign of Christ. So we clearly can see the bride has already been given to the groom before the Second Advent and the Millennium.

Others feel that the friends of the bride are the Old Testament saints. The question is asked, "Who else could they be?"

We need to understand that Jews and Gentiles who are saved must be a part of the bride of Christ.

So if the bride has already been given to the bridegroom, how could the Tribulation saints be a part of the bride?

John 14:2-3, "In my Father's house are many mansions: if it were not so, I would have told you. I go to prepare a place for you.

V3. And if I go and prepare a place for you, I will come again, and receive you unto myself; that where I am, there ye may be also."

He is talking about the Church.

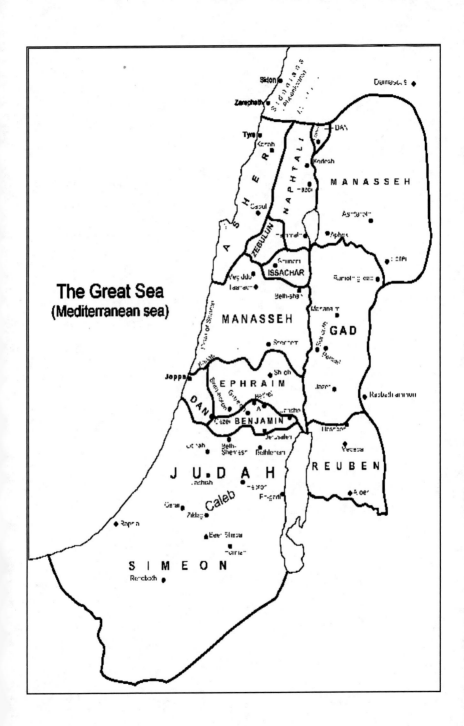

The Great Sea
(Mediterranean sea)

225

Chapter 21

THE NEW HEAVEN AND THE NEW EARTH

The New Jerusalem will be located in the new heaven and the new earth. The description of the New Jerusalem in Revelation chapter twenty-one includes its foundations, walls, gates, and streets. The length, breadth, and height of the city will be exactly twelve thousand furlongs (Revelation 21:16-17).

A furlong is a measurement of five hundred and eighty-two feet; therefore, the city will be one thousand, three hundred and twenty-three miles in every direction, giving it a total base area of one million, seven hundred and fifty thousand, three hundred and twenty-nine square miles, which has been estimated to house about seventy-two billion inhabitants.

Revelation twenty-one, verses ten through twenty-seven, gives a description of the new heaven and the new earth, along with the coming of the New Jerusalem. This of course will happen after the Millennial Reign of Christ, and after the White Throne Judgment.

Let's look at the description of the holy city.

Revelation 21:10-27, "And he carried me away in the spirit to a great and high mountain, and shewed me that great city, the holy Jerusalem, descending out of heaven from God,

V11. Having the glory of God: and her light was like unto a stone most precious, even like a jasper stone, clear as crystal;

V12. And had a wall great and high, and had twelve gates, and at the gates twelve angels, and names written thereon, which are the names of the twelve tribes of the children of

Israel:

V13.On the east three gates; on the north three gates; on the south three gates; and on the west three gates.

V14. And the wall of the city had twelve foundations, and in them the names of the twelve apostles of the Lamb.

V15. And he that talked with me had a golden reed to measure the city, and the gates thereof, and the wall thereof.

V16. And the city lieth foursquare, and the length is as large as the breadth: and he measured the city with the reed, twelve thousand furlongs. The length and the breadth and the height of it are equal.

V17. And he measured the wall thereof, an hundred and forty and four cubits, according to the measure of a man, that is, of the angel.

V18. And the building of the wall of it was of jasper: and the city was pure gold, like unto clear glass.

V19. And the foundations of the wall of the city were garnished with all manner of precious stones. The first foundation was jasper; the second, sapphire; the third, a chalcedony; the fourth, an emerald;

V20. The fifth, sardonyx; the sixth, sardius; the seventh, chrysolyte; the eighth, beryl; the ninth, a topaz; the tenth, a chrysoprasus; the eleventh, a jacinth; the twelfth, an amethyst.

V21. And the twelve gates were twelve pearls; every several gate was of one pearl: and the street of the city was pure gold, as it were transparent glass.

V22. And I saw no temple therein: for the Lord God Almighty and the Lamb are the temple of it.

V23. And the city had no need of the sun, neither of the moon, to shine in it: for the glory of God did lighten it, and the Lamb is the light thereof.

V24. And the nations of them which are saved shall walk in the light of it: and the kings of the earth do bring their glory and honour into it.

V25. And the gates of it shall not be shut at all by day: for there shall be no night there.

V26. And they shall bring the glory and honour of the nations into it.

V27. And there shall in no wise enter into it any thing that defileth, neither whatsoever worketh abomination, or maketh a lie: but they which are written in the Lamb's book of life."

In verse ten John saw the new city Jerusalem. In verse eleven he saw the city in all its glory.

In verse twelve he saw the great wall with twelve gates, and written on the gates were the names of the twelve tribes of Israel.

In verses thirteen and fourteen John saw that it was compassed about with a great wall, and on each of the four walls were three gates: one for each tribe of Israel. This wall had twelve foundations, one for each of the disciples.

In verses fifteen through seventeen the angel measured the holy city, the New Jerusalem.

In verses eighteen through twenty John saw the beauty of the walls.

In verse twenty-one he saw gates of pearl and streets of gold. In verses twenty-two and twenty-three he saw that there was no need for the sun or the moon, for God Himself will be its light.

In verse twenty-four he saw that in safety, peace, and glory men shall walk therein.

In verses twenty-five and twenty-six he saw that the gates of the city shall never be shut, and there shall be no night there.

In verse twenty-seven John saw that only those whose names were written in the Lamb's book of life were there.

Revelation 22:1-5, "And he shewed me a pure river of water of life, clear as crystal, proceeding out of the throne of God and of the Lamb.

V2. In the midst of the street of it, and on either side of the river, was there the tree of life, which bare twelve manner of fruits, and yielded her fruit every month: and the leaves of the tree were for the healing of the nations.

V3. And there shall be no more curse: but the throne of God and of the Lamb shall be in it; and his servants shall serve him:

V4. And they shall see his face; and his name shall be in their foreheads.

V5. And there shall be no night there; and they need no candle, neither light of the sun; for the Lord God giveth them light: and they shall reign for ever and ever."

In verse one there will be no pollution there.

In verse two we see the tree of life which yields its fruit every month, and bares twelve kinds of fruit.

In verse three God's throne will be there, and there will be no more curse.

In verse four we will see His face and bear His mark in our foreheads.

In verse five God will lighten our way.

I believe with all my heart that our Lord Jesus Christ will soon break the eastern sky and receive His people to Himself, and the "whosoever will" will be home with Him. It is important that we teach this because many will be left behind.

It is possible that they could be saved during the time of the Tribulation, provided that they had never rejected the Gospel of salvation. However, if you have heard the Gospel and have rejected it, as I have stated earlier, you will believe the great delusion, and be lost forever.

Revelation 21:22, "And I saw no temple therein: for the Lord God Almighty and the Lamb are the temple of it."

This new creation will be part of the new world which will be created after the present heaven and earth are destroyed by fire at the end of history (2Pet. 3:10-13). The New Jerusalem will be the eternal home of the bride and the inhabitants of the New Jerusalem will include angels, the Church, God (the judge), and Christ (the mediator). Some believe that the Old Testament saints will live there also, and others teach that only the New Testament saints will dwell there while the Old Testament saints will dwell on the new earth.

Some believe the Old Testament saints are not part of the bride, but are only friends of the bridegroom (John 3:29), and therefore only the New Testament Church can be part of the bride. What do you think? It's wonderful to know, one day, and I believe soon, we will be with our LORD and know all things.

John 3:29, "He that hath the bride is the bridegroom: but the friend of the bridegroom, which standeth and heareth him, rejoiceth greatly because of the bridegroom's voice: this my joy therefore is fulfilled."

If a person says they know the meaning of every Scripture of prophecy in God's Word, well, you fill in the blank.

Revelation, 21:24, "And the nations of them which are saved shall walk in the light of it: and the kings of the earth do bring their glory and honour into it."

Most believe the conditions found in the Garden of Eden will return along with the time of innocence. Adam and Eve had lived in perfect, peaceful harmony with God. Yet from the moment of their rebellion against God man has lived under a curse.

The apostle Paul prophesied concerning the redemption of all creation.

In Romans 8:21 he wrote: *"Because the creature itself also shall be delivered from the bondage of corruption into the glorious liberty of the children of God."*

The universe is affected by sin in both the spiritual and material realms; but the ultimate deliverance will occur after the millennial and the last judgment found in Revelation twenty, when God makes all things new.

This is not the end but the New Beginning.

Psalms 126:5-6

Bibles and Commentaries:

The King James Study Bible
Matthew Henry's Study Bible
Nave's Topical Bible
Scofield Study Bible

Sermons and Articles:

Dr. H.A. Ironside
Dr. Oliver B. Greene
Dr. Charles Spurgeon
Dr. Harold Sightler
Dr. Hal Lindsey
Dr. Clarence Larkin

Bible Dictionaries:

Matthew Henry's Commentary of the Whole Bible
Easton's Bible Dictionary
Smith's Bible Dictionary

All Scripture quotes in this book are from the Authorized King James Version of the Bible.